Population Growth and Economic Development: Policy Questions

Working Group on Population Growth
and Economic Development

Committee on Population

Commission on Behavioral and
Social Sciences and Education

National Research Council

NATIONAL ACADEMY PRESS
Washington, D.C. 1986

NATIONAL ACADEMY PRESS   2101 Constitution Avenue NW   Washington, DC 20418

Library of Congress Cataloging-in-Publication Data

Population growth and economic development.

 Bibliography: p.
 Includes index.
 1. Developing countries—Population. 2. Developing countries—Economic conditions. I. National Research Council (U.S.). Working Group on Population Growth and Economic Development.
 HB884.P6655   1986   304.6'09172'4   86-862
 ISBN 0-309-03641-0

Cover photograph © Don Rutledge, Taurus Photos, Inc.

We gratefully acknowledge the assistance we received from the TyX Corporation, Reston, Virginia, which provided access to electronic pagination and laser-printer technology for producing camera copy.

Printed in the United States of America.

First Printing, March 1986
Second Printing, July 1988
Third Printing, December 1989
Fourth Printing, November 1990
Fifth Printing, October 1991

Working Group on Population Growth and Economic Development

D. GALE JOHNSON (*Cochair*), Department of Economics, University of Chicago

RONALD D. LEE (*Cochair*), Graduate Group in Demography, University of California, Berkeley

NANCY BIRDSALL, Population, Health, and Nutrition Department, The World Bank, Washington, D.C.

RODOLFO A. BULATAO, Population, Health, and Nutrition Department, The World Bank, Washington, D.C.

EVA MUELLER, Population Studies Center, University of Michigan

SAMUEL H. PRESTON, Population Studies Center, University of Pennsylvania

T. PAUL SCHULTZ, Department of Economics, Yale University

T. N. SRINÍVASAN, Department of Economics, Yale University

ANNE D. WILLIAMS, Department of Economics, Bates College

KENNETH M. CHOMITZ, National Research Council Fellow

GEOFFREY GREENE, Research Associate

Contents

Preface

This report summarizes evidence on the relationships between population growth and economic development, concentrating on the developing nations. Following an introduction that sets forth the problem, the report addresses nine relevant and currently debated major questions bearing on these relationships and then summarizes the conclusions in a final chapter.

In 1963 the Panel on Population Problems of the Committee on Science and Public Policy of the National Academy of Sciences published a report entitled *The Growth of World Population*. The appointment of that panel and the publication of its report were expressions of concern then felt by scientists, as well as by other informed persons in many countries, about the implications of population trends. At that time, the most consequential trend was the pronounced and long-continued acceleration in the rate of increase of the population of the world, especially in the poorer countries. It was estimated in 1963 that the annual rate of increase of the global population had reached 2 percent, a rate that would lead to a doubling of the population every 35 years. The disproportionate contribution of low-income areas to that acceleration was caused by rapid declines in mortality combined with high fertility that remained almost unchanged.

Since 1963, however, the peak of the rate of growth in the world's population has been passed. A dramatic decline in the birth rate in almost all the developed countries has lowered their aggregate annual rate of increase to well below 1 percent, and the rate of increase has also declined in the developing countries as a whole. In some low-income areas, a sharp decline in fertility has more than offset the growth-inducing effect of the generally continued reduction in the death rate, although the rate of population increase remains high in many developing countries.

Debate continued about the relationships between population growth and economic development. The National Academy of Sciences, through a study committee of the Office of the Foreign Secretary chaired by Roger Revelle, and with support from the Agency for International Development (AID), examined the issue and in 1971 published a two-volume report entitled *Rapid Population Growth: Consequences and Policy Implications*.

A dozen years later, in response to the ongoing debate about population growth, associated especially with the publication of several major works discussed in the introduction to this report, AID again asked the Academy to undertake an assessment. The Rockefeller Foundation and the William and Flora Hewlett Foundation also supported the work, as did the National Academy of Sciences and the National Academy of Engineering through the NRC Fund.* With this support, the report presented here was prepared by the Working Group on Population Growth and Economic Development of the Committee on Population. The report follows a series of publications by the predecessor Committee on Population and Demography, which evaluated evidence on levels and trends of fertility and mortality in selected developing nations, worked on the improvement of technologies for estimating fertility and mortality where only incomplete or inadequate data existed, and evaluated the factors determining the changes in birth rates in developing countries. (A list of reports produced under this work program is found on the inside back cover.)

This report considers the consequences of population growth for economic systems. Historically, the issue originated as one of concern for the deleterious consequences of rapid population growth: some analysts clearly saw disaster in the offing if the then-current rates of growth continued; others saw no problem at all. Those positions—which might be called the extreme environmentalist and extreme mercantilist views—are considered herein, as well as the more moderate positions favored by many scholars. This report finds little support for either the most alarmist or the most complacent views concerning the economic effects of population growth.

The Working Group on Population Growth and Economic Development

---

*The National Research Council (NRC) Fund is a pool of private, discretionary, nonfederal funds that is used to support a program of Academy-initiated studies of national issues in which science and technology figure significantly. The NRC Fund consists of contributions from a consortium of private foundations including the Carnegie Corporation of New York, the Charles E. Culpeper Foundation, the William and Flora Hewlett Foundation, the John D. and Catherine T. MacArthur Foundation, the Andrew W. Mellon Foundation, the Rockefeller Foundation, and the Alfred P. Sloan Foundation; the Academy Industry Program, which seeks annual contributions from companies that are concerned with the health of U.S. science and technology and with public policy issues with technological content; and the National Academy of Sciences and the National Academy of Engineering endowments.

also commissioned a group of background papers that cover in technical detail the topics summarized here; these are cited throughout. In addition, a second activity of the Committee on Population, the Working Group on Family Planning Effectiveness, is completing a major assessment on what is known about the operation and management of family planning programs in the developing world.

In carrying out its mandate, the Working Group on Population Growth and Economic Development met several times and conducted a workshop to review early drafts of background papers and to begin to synthesize the findings for this report. Several authors of the papers attended the workshop along with working group members. The committee and the National Research Council are grateful to these authors and especially to the members of the working group for their diligence in struggling with complex issues. All the working group members contributed ideas and reactions as the report progressed through many drafts. Particular appreciation is due to working group member Samuel Preston, who had principal responsibility for the initial drafting of the report; to cochair Ronald D. Lee and research associate Geoffrey Greene, who were also instrumental in early drafts of the report; and to Kenneth M. Chomitz, NRC fellow, who assisted with the drafting and coordination of the final text.

Thanks are also expressed to the other members of the committee staff, who helped organize the working group and provided necessary support throughout the project. These include Robert J. Lapham and Peter J. Donaldson, study directors at the beginning and end of the project; Diane Lindley, research assistant; and Cheryl Hailey, administrative secretary. In addition, Eugenia Grohman, associate director for reports of the Commission on Behavioral and Social Sciences and Education, and Elaine McGarraugh, production editor, applied their unusual editorial talents to the report.

The committee is grateful to all the working group members and committee staff for their efforts on this report.

Eugene Hammel, *Chair*
Committee on Population

Population
Growth and
Economic
Development:
Policy
Questions

Introduction

BACKGROUND

In 1984 there were approximately 3.6 billion people living in the developing regions of the world, conventionally defined as comprising Africa, Latin America, and Asia except Japan. This number was growing annually at a rate of about 2.0 percent (United Nations, 1984:101). For every 1,000 persons, there were 31.2 births and 11.0 deaths. Under estimated rates of childbearing in 1980-1985, each woman in developing countries would bear an average of 4.1 children if she survived to the end of her reproductive years. Based on age-specific mortality rates in 1980-1985, a newborn could expect to live 56.6 years (United Nations, 1985:144).

These numbers represent a substantial change in demographic conditions during the postwar period. In 1950 there were only 1.7 billion people living in the developing countries. Under 1950-1955 rates, women were bearing an average of 6.2 children, and newborns could expect to live only 41.0 years (United Nations, 1985:144). There were 45.4 births and 24.4 deaths annually per 1,000 persons.

The only important similarity to the situation three decades later was the rate of population growth: 2.1 percent annually in 1950-1955, and 2.0 percent in 1980-1985. However, there was a rise to an annual rate of 2.55 percent in 1965-1970 and a subsequent decline. This hill-shaped pattern of population growth rates is not so pronounced if China is excluded from the calculations: without China, annual growth rates for the less-developed countries were 2.1 percent in 1950-1955, 2.5 percent in 1965-1970, and 2.4

1

percent in 1980-1984. Recent demographic estimates for major areas of the developing world are presented in Table 1.

Sustained population growth rates of this magnitude are unprecedented in history and reflect above all human success in reducing the burden of premature and avoidable death in developing countries. The growth rates are nearly twice those in industrialized areas of Europe during the nineteenth century. Despite being indicators of success, the high rates of population growth in developing countries during the postwar period have caused concern, and the focus of attention has been on the social and economic costs of high levels of fertility.

To many observers, these costs have appeared obvious. The earth's resources are finite, and more people by definition means fewer natural resources per person. Of course, the most important resources are not natural, but artificial (plants and equipment used in production, openings in school systems, jobs, social institutions, and economic infrastructure) and so are expandable. But human beings begin life with an extended period of dependency during which they contribute nothing to the production of these resources, while calling on them for sustenance and development. In the short term, at least, it appears obvious that all resources will be spread more thinly if there are more children. In the era of rapid population growth, the stage of childhood dependency came to be perceived as a burden with which families and societies must cope. Thus, population growth (i.e., high fertility) took its place alongside other self-evident problems such as crime, disease, illiteracy, hunger, and poverty, to be dealt with by informed social policy.

Because the costs of population growth seemed self-evident, following directly from the fixity of nature and the long period required for a newly born child to become fully productive, the issue was not the subject of a great deal of research. National policies were based on commonsense impressions; in 1952, India became the first country to initiate a family planning program.

Among early studies that took a more systematic approach to population matters was a 1958 book by Ansley Coale and Edgar Hoover, *Population Growth and Economic Development in Low-Income Countries*, and a report and series of papers commissioned by the National Academy of Sciences (1971), *Rapid Population Growth: Consequences and Policy Implications*. The former focused on the effects of population growth and associated high burdens of dependency on rates of physical capital formation, using Mexico and India for illustrative purposes. The latter was perhaps most noteworthy for introducing issues relating to the effect of population growth on human capital formation, which research subsequent to Coale and Hoover's book had shown to be a major element in economic growth. Both studies concluded that rapid population growth had seriously negative economic consequences.

TABLE 1 Estimates of Demographic Variables for Major World Regions

Region	1985 Population (in millions)	Annual Percentage Growth Rate		Crude Birth Rate per 1,000		Crude Death Rate per 1,000		Total Fertility Rate per 1,000		Life Expectancy at Birth		Percentage of Population under 15	
		1950-1955	1980-1985	1950-1955	1980-1985	1950-1955	1980-1985	1950-1955	1980-1985	1950-1955	1980-1985	1955	1985
Sub-Saharan Africa	449.8	2.00	3.03	48.0	47.6	28.0	17.5	6.4	6.6	36.4	47.9	42.7	46.1
Latin America	406.2	2.72	2.30	42.5	31.8	15.5	8.2	5.9	4.1	51.0	64.1	40.5	38.0
East Asia and Pacific (except Japan)	1,498.9	2.07	1.40	44.8	21.8	24.1	7.7	5.9	2.8	41.1	64.8	36.5	32.6
South Asia	1,052.6	1.86	2.16	45.7	35.7	27.0	14.0	6.6	4.8	39.0	51.6	40.2	39.2
Middle East and North Africa	180.9	2.64	2.98	50.5	42.3	23.0	12.3	7.2	6.1	43.6	57.0	41.3	43.3
Total Developing Regions	3,763.4	2.10	2.00	45.0	31.0	24.0	11.0	6.1	4.1	41.4	56.9	38.6	37.2
Industrial Market Economies	734.8	1.19	0.53	21.2	14.0	10.2	9.5	2.8	1.8	67.4	74.5	27.0	20.9
East European Non-market Economies	394.4	1.49	0.85	25.5	18.2	9.9	9.7	2.9	2.3	62.1	71.1	29.0	24.5
Southern Europe	94.2	1.73	1.55	33.4	25.1	13.0	9.1	4.4	3.4	55.0	67.1	33.3	30.7

Source: United Nations (1985) medium variant projections, aggregated to geographical regions defined in World Bank (1983a:xxxiii-xxxv).

At one point, the Academy report argued (National Academy of Sciences, 1971, Vol. 1:29):

> If the less developed regions could raise their current per capita income growth rates by one-third, it would reduce their per capita income doubling time from somewhat over 25 years to 18 years. Under current circumstances this could be accomplished entirely through a fall of the average birth rate in the less developed region from their roughly 40 per 1,000 level to 30 per 1,000, a 25 percent shift, which, in addition to its income effects, could have perhaps equally large family-welfare effects not captured by conventional income measures.

Elaborate but essentially mechanical modeling exercises, such as *Limits to Growth* (Meadows et al., 1972), which incorporated fixed factors of production and fixed absorptive capacity of the environment in combination with projected rises in population, seemed to confirm that there was much to fear about population growth. This pessimistic view was vividly presented in the widely publicized *Global 2000 Report to the President* (Council on Environmental Quality and U.S. Department of State, 1980).

But it is clear that despite rapid population growth, developing countries have achieved unprecedented levels of income per capita, literacy, and life expectancy over the past 25 years (see Table 2). Furthermore, as recognized in the earlier Academy report, there is no statistical association between national rates of population growth and growth rates of income per capita. These observations point toward the key mediating role that human behavior and human institutions play in the relation between population growth and economic processes, a role that has been acknowledged for some time by economists and demographers (National Academy of Sciences, 1971, Vol. 1:65; Berelson, 1975:3).

For example, as easily accessible reserves of important natural resources are exhausted, the real cost of extraction, and hence the resource price, rises. In turn, this tends to stimulate the search for new processes that use the resource more efficiently, for improved extraction techniques, for new sources, and for less expensive substitutes. In this manner, the response of the economic system to scarcity tends to weaken the direct effect of population growth on resources. Perhaps more important, it is obvious that most parents are willing to make many of the sacrifices required to raise a child through its dependency period, so that some of the most important economic adjustments to population growth are not only automatic but even considered part of a desirable process by those who undertake them. Recognition that human institutions, especially the family, play an important role in adaptations to population growth led to considerable attention being focused on the microeconomics of household decisions regarding work, childbearing, and investments in children (e.g., Easterlin, 1980).

TABLE 2 Economic Indicators for Major World Regions

Region	Annual Growth Rate of Real GDP/Capita				Persons per Physician		Calories per Capita as Percentage of Requirements		Adult Literacy (percent)		Secondary Education Enrollment Ratio		Urban Population (percent)	
	1950-1960	1960-1965	1965-1970	1970-1981	1960	MRE[a]	1960	MRE[a]	1960	MRE[a]	1960	MRE[a]	1960	MRE[a]
Sub-Saharan Africa	1.2	2.7	2.3	0.4	49,470	21,120	92.7	92.3	15.7	42.9	3.6	14.4	13.9	23.6
Latin America and Caribbean	1.9	2.0	3.4	2.7	2,560	1,810	107.3	111.0	64.8	79.0	14.0	38.6	49.4	65.8
East Asia and Pacific (except Japan)	2.7[b]	3.0[b]	5.5[b]	5.6[b]	12,420	3,550	81.9	108.4	53.2[b]	69.6	19.4	36.0	20.5[b]	28.8[b]
South Asia	2.0	1.9	2.5	1.6	7,000	4,440	95.1	89.3	27.6	35.3	17.4	25.2	16.8	22.8
Middle East and North Africa	1.8	1.3	3.1	4.1	10,520	3,550	94.8	102.3	18.3	43.3	12.8	41.9	33.8	47.5
Total Developing Regions	2.4	2.6	3.5	2.8	13,770	5,710	91.2	101.5	38.8[b]	55.5	16.6	31.6	23.6[b]	33.2[b]
Industrial Market Economies	3.0	4.0	3.8	2.3	820	550	125.5	134.4	96.0	98.9	63.9	89.2	68.1	78.2
East European Non-market Economies	NA	NA	NA	NA	680	350	128.8	132.9	97.1	99.4	45.2	92.0	48.3	61.7
Southern Europe	4.1	4.9	5.1	3.3	1,920	1,100	119.8	129.6	55.2	69.7	33.1	56.5	31.7	47.8

[a]Most recent estimate.
[b]Not including China.

Sources: Growth rate of gross domestic product (GDP) per capita: World Bank (1983a:486); other statistics: World Bank (1983b:148, 149, 158, 159).

A more provocative challenge to conventional wisdom was posed by Julian Simon's 1981 book, *The Ultimate Resource,* which argued that population is an important long-term stimulus to economic advance through its effects on productive technology, the pace of innovation, the formation of markets, and governmental infrastructural investments. Simon's book received a good deal of both scholarly and popular attention and has been influential in U.S. policy. The pace of research on consequences of population growth accelerated with the approach of the 1984 World Population Conference in Mexico City, held under the auspices of the United Nations. In addition, several papers on the economic consequences of population growth, including an important one by McNicoll (1984), were commissioned by the World Bank in preparation for its *World Development Report* special 1984 issue on population.

FOCUS ON FERTILITY DECLINE AND ECONOMIC WELFARE

Against this background, the National Research Council undertook an extensive effort to synthesize knowledge on the economic consequences of population growth. This volume represents a summary of much recent research on the economic consequences of population growth in developing countries, including the 17 papers commissioned by the working group on important aspects of economic-demographic relations. The report is organized in terms of the major questions around which discussion has focused. The questions are not mutually exclusive and are perhaps best evaluated in toto rather than individually. But the subject is large, and some organizing framework is necessary.

One important finding of the report is that the evidence regarding the consequences of a change in the rate of population growth is extremely varied, some arguments coming from theory and some from empirical studies. Furthermore, those studies differ widely in quality and scope. Drawing firm conclusions about the overall impact of slower population growth is difficult because the research completed to date is frequently based on limited samples and inadequate data as well as on partial and occasionally inappropriate conceptual models and statistical techniques. The scientific literature contains few adequate studies of the effects of slower population growth in developed countries and fewer still on the effects in developing countries. Consequently, there is much less certainty than we would like about the specific quantifiable effects of different rates of population growth on human capital formation, on physical capital formation in firms, on technical progress and its diffusion, and on the numerous other questions that are addressed in the following chapters.

As in the 1971 Academy volumes, we focus on the effects of a slowing of a population's growth due to a policy-driven fertility decline. Although population growth depends on migration and mortality as well as fertility, for most developing countries–and surely for the developing world as a whole– there is little potential for major changes in population growth rates or sizes as a result of international migration. And certainly, regardless of economic consequences, public policies will continue to strive for improvements in public health and access to medical care, which will result in continuing mortality decreases and longer life expectancy. Hence, the greatest discretionary scope for altering population growth rates to achieve economic aims rests with fertility policy, and so we have focused on fertility in establishing a framework for considering population policy.

In considering the consequences of fertility decline, we focus on measures of economic well-being or welfare. In particular, we emphasize variables that are closely related to levels of per capita income, which is a widely recognized indicator of economic welfare. Such variables as capital per worker and land per person concern us mainly because they are directly linked to per capita income. However, we recognize that per capita income is not identical to well-being; individuals can often improve their well-being by sacrificing per capita family income for other goods such as leisure or children. While we also give some consideration to other major objects of social and economic policy–namely, the distribution of income and levels of health and education–we were not able to consider broader measures of well-being, and we make only passing references to such development concerns as interest rates, foreign exchange regimes, or industrial structure.

UNDERSTANDING THE CONSEQUENCES
OF FERTILITY DECLINE

Population growth and economic development are complex, interlinked processes. Each affects the other in many ways, and both are interrelated to the broad array of social and political changes that constitute modernization. Consequently, simple correlations between population growth and per capita income, although intriguing, ultimately provide little insight into the causal impact of a policy-driven decline in fertility. A scientific assessment of that impact requires that one identify the major mechanisms by which population growth is hypothesized to affect economic development; assess the evidence for each hypothesis; and, finally, synthesize the net effect of the simultaneous operation of these mechanisms.

A starting point in this assessment is to recognize several demographic changes that follow automatically from a permanent reduction in the number of children born per woman of childbearing age if there is no change in mortality:

- The population will grow more slowly than it would otherwise have grown.
- At every time subsequent to the fertility reduction, the population will be smaller than it would have been.
- At every subsequent time, the population will be less dense than it would have been (having fewer persons per square mile).
- At every subsequent time, the population will have an age structure that is older than it would have been. It will have a smaller proportion of children, a larger proportion of the elderly, and an older mean age.

All of these short- and long-run demographic changes are in the same direction; however, the short- and long-run responses may differ in the rate of change of population growth and the age distribution.

In a population with constant age-specific mortality and constant age-specific fertility that undergoes a sudden and permanent change to a lower level of age-specific fertility, all the above-mentioned effects will be observed. But eventually, after a transitional period of two to three generations (or roughly 70 years) the population will settle down to a new demographic equilibrium. The rate of growth, while lower than it would have been, will no longer be declining, and the average age of the population will have stabilized at an older mean age. Certain economic responses that may be observed during this transitional period will not continue once the new population growth pattern has been attained. But even though many economic effects occur only during this transitional period, they can result in higher or lower endowments of technology, capital, and natural resources for future generations. (If the effect of a policy-induced fertility reduction is to hasten a decline that would in any case have occurred later, the first and last effects noted above are transitory, while the second and third are still generally true.)

These demographic changes, both short and long term, are hypothesized to affect economic welfare through a variety of mechanisms, as noted above. We have identified the most important of these hypotheses and organized them as a set of questions that refer to both transitory and permanent effects:

1. Will slower population growth increase the growth rate of per capita income through increasing per capita availability of exhaustible resources?

2. Will slower population growth increase the growth rate of per capita income through increasing per capita availability of renewable resources?

3. Will slower population growth alleviate pollution and the degradation of the natural environment?

4. Will slower population growth lead to more capital per worker, thereby increasing per worker output and consumption?

5. Do lower population densities lead to lower per capita incomes via a reduced stimulus to technological innovation and reduced exploitation of economies of scale in production and infrastructure?

6. Will slower population growth increase per capita levels of schooling and health?

7. Will slower population growth decrease the degree of inequality in the distribution of income?

8. Will slower population growth facilitate the absorption of workers into the modern economic sector and alleviate problems of urban growth?

9. Does a couple's fertility behavior impose costs on society at large?

For the first eight questions, we examine both the theoretical rationale for the hypothesis and the empirical evidence that bears upon it. Because we are interested in the dynamic effects of population growth, historical and time-series data are of special interest. However, historical studies, particularly of only one country, have two possible drawbacks: first, underlying relationships may have changed over time so that the historical data are no longer relevant; second, the experience of any particular country may not be representative or generalizable. Moreover, historical information may simply be lacking. When possible, then, we also draw on recent comparisons of countries with different population sizes, densities, or growth rates. If confounding variables can be controlled, these cross-national comparisons can be interpreted as natural experiments in the effects of population variables. However, it is more difficult to control for background variables in cross-sectional than in time-series analyses. The two perspectives are therefore complementary.

The final question is somewhat different in form from the other eight. Based primarily on theoretical arguments, it introduces the important distinction between private and social consequences of childbearing decisions. This distinction reflects differences between the childbearing costs and benefits realized by the couple making the childbearing decisions and those realized by the society at large. This question is especially important in social decision making, since the argument for social intervention in population matters is much stronger if the costs and benefits are shown to fall heavily on people not involved in childbearing decisions.

While we provide a general framework for studying the population-economic interrelationship in developing countries, it must be understood that conditions vary quite dramatically from place to place. Temperate South America is highly urbanized and has income levels that are high by historical standards. Most people in Asia live in quite dense agrarian areas where income levels are very low. Much of Africa is also poor but has low population density and uses very different agricultural techniques than Asia. Many Middle Eastern countries are land-poor but resource-rich with oil. The importance of these and other differences emerges in our review, but it should be borne in mind throughout that we are not attempting to provide answers that pertain to all times and places.

It should also be stressed that although the future contains many features that are essentially unknowable, one pertinent feature can be seen in sharp outline and is almost certain to distinguish the future from the past: populations will be substantially larger in developing countries than ever before. According to the United Nation's medium variant projections of 1982, the population of the developing world will reach 6.8 billion by 2025–an 89 percent increase over the 1985 level. This is ensured (barring catastrophe) because of the young age structure of these populations. The population in the middle and older age groups is certain to grow even if fertility declines are rapid enough to offset the growing number of reproductive-aged persons and keep the child population from growing. Even though population growth rates are declining in many developing countries, they seem almost certain to remain high relative to growth rates in the developed countries during comparable periods of their economic history.

1 Will slower population growth increase the growth rate of per capita income through increasing per capita availability of exhaustible resources?

MARKETS AND NATURAL RESOURCE PRICES

In contrast to resources like agricultural land that can, in principle, remain productive in perpetuity if properly managed, the earth's crust has a finite supply of such resources as fossil fuels and nonfuel minerals. These resources are partially destroyed, or at least substantially transformed, in the production and consumption of the economic goods and services that use them, so that the world's stock declines. Although recycling can partly offset this decline—for example, the world steel industry now uses scrap iron to satisfy 45 percent of its iron requirements (Chandler, 1984)—for practical purposes, the potential flow of economic services from exhaustible resources is limited because the stock is finite.

Perhaps because of the evident scarcity of the earth's resources, institutions governing property rights to the most important exhaustible resources have a long history. Market mechanisms are the most important institutions for allocating resources among users, and even in societies with nonmarket economic systems, world market conditions exert an important influence on resource allocation decisions. Market prices, then, are important in determining how resources are used, including how much is retained for future use.

The market price of an exhaustible resource is determined by both supply and demand. Demand for a resource is derived from the demand for the goods it is used to produce. The derived demand therefore depends on population, income level, the relative price of the goods, and the technological feasibility

11

and price of substitutes for either the resource or the goods. If other things are constant, an increase in either population or income will tend to boost the demand for a resource, though the demand for some goods will be more sensitive to population and the demand for others more sensitive to income.

On the supply side, there are two components to producers' costs. Extraction costs reflect the labor and capital required to supply a unit of the resource for production, which generally increases as the stock of the resource declines, although improvements in extraction technology may slow the rate of the increase. For example, the development of heavy earth-moving equipment reduced the price of copper by making it easier to extract lower ore grades (Slade, 1985). The other component of producers' cost of a resource reflects the rate of return to the resource stock considered as a capital asset, comparable to a market interest rate. Thus, if there is an increase in the expected future demand for a good requiring the resource, the value of the economic services that can be provided by the resource stock will also increase, an implicit capital gain that will be reflected in the rate-of-return component of the market price.

Current and expected future prices drive the search for additional reserves of a resource, for substitutes, and for conservation measures. There is reasonably good evidence that the availability of many resources is quite sensitive to price. For example, the U.S. Bureau of Mines has estimated that domestic mercury reserves are 1,600 metric tons if the price is $2,900/ton but are 50,000 metric tons if the price is $43,500/ton (Goeller and Zucker, 1984). Conservation and substitution activities are also price sensitive, as evidenced by reactions to the increase in fossil fuel prices during the 1970s. In both developed and developing countries, the growth in energy inputs required for production had declined sharply by the latter part of the decade (MacKellar and Vining, 1985). Similarly, in 1972, U.S. annual energy consumption was projected to be 160 quads (a unit of energy) by the year 2000, but in 1982 that projection was only 95 quads (Firor and Portney, 1982:200). When Zaire, producer of more than half of the world's supply of cobalt, reduced its allotments to customers by 30 percent, prices rose from $11/kg to $35/kg. But this price increase led to such extensive introduction of substitutes (e.g., manganese and lead in paints) that U.S. consumption of cobalt in turn fell by one-half (Goeller and Zucker, 1984).

In a setting with perfect competition and perfect capital markets, whose participants accurately anticipate future supply and demand conditions, prices will efficiently allocate resources among alternative uses and over time, in the sense that no individual in any generation could be made better off without someone else being made worse off. In formulations that demonstrate this result, future prices are discounted at the market rate of interest, which incorporates the premium that must be paid to agents to defer current consumption until some point in the future (Smith and Krutilla, 1979). In this context, since the current price of an exhaustible resource reflects the fact that the stock is an asset that could be sold at a capital gain in the future, the resource will be depleted optimally.

Of course, the conditions ensuring intertemporally efficient resource allocations are unlikely to be satisfied precisely. Particularly unrealistic is the condition of perfect foresight–that current market participants correctly anticipate the future course of supply and demand so that the spot price of a resource at any time is linked to all future prices. It is through this indirect mechanism that future generations are represented in the market, since a high anticipated future price increases the current value of a resource stock, also increasing the current price. To the extent that present-day speculators underestimate future demand, stocks will be drawn down too rapidly (and conversely for overestimates of future demand).

It is debatable whether government perceptions of future supply and demand can be more accurate than market perceptions, a condition that would justify government intervention. Long-run predictions are clearly difficult. Reflection on the past century's economic history suggests that unanticipated changes in tastes and technology drastically shifted the configuration of "essential" resources. Such shifts in the future, combined with capital market imperfections, would result in inefficient intertemporal allocation of resource consumption, though it is impossible to predict a priori whether the result would be overconservation or underconservation.

Monopoly is another source of market failure. Because of the geological processes that produced them, some fuel and nonfuel minerals may be concentrated geographically so that stocks may be held by relatively few organizations or countries. For example, while world coal deposits are relatively uniformly distributed, oil deposits are not (MacKellar and Vining, 1985). When the stock of an exhaustible resource is monopolistically controlled, the market price will be higher than it would be under more competition. Because a higher price will result in decreased demand, if all else is equal, the effect of monopolistic distortions will tend to bias intertemporal allocations toward resource conservation (Dasgupta and Heal, 1979).

But despite these imperfections, many economists believe that actual markets come closer to producing such an efficient outcome than any other institution and that results in actual markets tend toward or approximate the results obtained in the pure case (Stiglitz, 1979; Dasgupta and Heal, 1979). For example, when the Organization of Petroleum Exporting Countries (OPEC) cartel imposed oil price increases in the 1970s, the ensuing expansion of supply, substitution of alternative energy sources such as natural gas and coal, and conservation measures reduced the demand for OPEC oil enough to significantly diminish the cartel's price-setting power.

The physical characteristics of a resource may make property rights difficult to define practically, potentially distorting the efficiency of markets. But when a resource is economically important, there are powerful incentives to establish effective rules governing access to it through negotiation or other social institutions. For example, underground oil reservoirs may extend beneath land owned by many different persons or agencies. To maximize individual revenues, each individual oil producer would be motivated to pump oil as rapidly as possible, even though this would damage the deposit and reduce the total amount available for extraction. Despite the difficulties of establishing ownership rights to the pool itself, oil producers and governments have constructed elaborate systems of allocating a particular field among claimants that approximate the efficient market outcome (Dasgupta and Heal, 1979).

To summarize, because virtually all economically important exhaustible resources are allocated by markets or by nonmarket social institutions that approximate market processes, the increasing physical scarcity of a resource will be reflected in increases in its price. In turn, price increases tend to stimulate conservation, improvements in extraction technology, and the search for less expensive substitutes. If these responses are successful, the resource becomes economically less scarce, tending to stem price increases. Thus, the absence of any long-term trends toward increasing real prices of exhaustible resources has been interpreted as contradicting the hypothesis of growing scarcity (Simon, 1981; Simon and Kahn, 1984; Barnett et al., 1984), although others find some evidence of a U-shaped price trend attributable to increasing extraction costs (Slade, 1982). For instance, iron, copper, and silver declined in price over the period 1890-1930, but have risen since. Aluminum trended downward over 1890-1980, and tin upward, while lead and zinc remained constant (Slade, 1982).

Exhaustible resource depletion does not seem likely to constrain world economic growth in the foreseeable future. Nonfuel minerals represent only 1.2 percent of the total value of world production (Goeller and Zucker, 1984), and a long-term resource requirement study suggests that depletion of significant nonfuel mineral resources is unlikely (Leontief et al., 1983). The heavy dependency of the world economy on conventional petroleum resources may pose a more immediate risk, but the potential supply of nonconventional petroleum from sources such as oil shale, and from relatively close substitutes for oil, such as coal and gas, is immense (MacKellar and Vining, 1985). Ultimately, the depletion of energy resources will continue until it becomes economical to rely directly on sunlight, an inexhaustible source of energy. This time may come sooner than formerly believed because of technical advances in the production of photovoltaic cells (Flavin and

Postel, 1984), although there are also more skeptical views on the ability of direct solar power to satisfy the energy requirements of current, energy-intensive technology (Beckmann, 1984).

POPULATION AND EXHAUSTIBLE RESOURCES

Although the central focus of this report is the impact of population growth at the country level, the scope of this discussion of exhaustible resources is at a global level because of the nature of resources. The extensive international trade in fossil energy and nonfuel mineral resources means that any effects of increased demand due to population growth in developing countries will be experienced in world markets, affecting all nations. For example, countries that are net exporters of resources may be worse off with a reduction in resource demand due to lower population growth, even if there is a global increase in consumption per head. And globally efficient resource use may involve international agreements on taxes, subsidies, and transfers. With continuing depletion, the global stock of a finite resource will vanish. The rate at which the stock is depleted depends on the rate of population growth, income levels, and perhaps most important, on the success of the price-induced search for more efficient ways to extract and use the resource in the production of goods for final consumption.

The rate of population growth, in itself, bears no necessary relationship to the rate of depletion. Indeed, the fact that exhaustible resource consumption is highest in economies with high income levels (Slade, 1985) means that the trends in demand for resources in developed countries may be much more important in determining the rate of global resource use than the trends in developing countries. Furthermore, a world with a regime of very rapid population growth but slow increases in income might experience slower resource depletion than one with a stationary population but rapid increases in income. Moreover, even if slower population growth does delay the time at which a particular stage of resource depletion is reached, which seems likely, it has no necessary or even probable effect on the number of people who will live under a particular stage of resource depletion. Under the implausible assumption (for the reason given above; also see Koopmans [1974]) of constant per capita resource use up to the point of resource exhaustion, the rate of population growth has no effect on the number of persons who are able to use a resource, although it does, of course, advance the date at which exhaustion occurs. Approximately the same result would hold under other, more plausible regimes in which price effects are introduced. Unless one is more concerned with the welfare of people born in the distant future than those born in the immediate future, there is little reason to be concerned about the rate at which population growth is depleting the stock of exhaustible resources.

An objection to this argument is that by slowing population growth, societies can "buy time" and prepare for a particular stage of resource depletion. Presumably, technological development might occur that would relieve pressure on the resource by providing substitutes or by enhancing its productivity. This possibility cannot be completely discounted, but it assumes that the technological development will occur in a manner exogenous to the supply and demand circumstances in the market for the resource. Many analysts find evidence that inventive effort of this kind is spurred primarily by expected profitability (e.g., Gould, 1972:Chapter 5), but serendipitous technological changes surely do occur that are essentially knowledge driven rather than market driven. For any particular country, in fact, most of the change in resource use will be exogenous to its own market and, hence, population size. A country thus may have an incentive to reduce its growth rate so that more people will live under the superior technological (but depleted resources) environment of the future. Such considerations involve comparisons of rates of technological change and resource depletion, as well as complex international relations in resource use, including the effects of one nation's behavior on the well-being of other nations. Since all economically important exhaustible resources are traded in international markets, one can have a clearer view with a global approach. Here, it seems likely that the principal route for technological advance in resource use is for increased scarcity, as signaled by increasing market prices, to stimulate a search for economizing strategies.

CONCLUSIONS

The scarcity of exhaustible resources is at most a minor constraint on economic growth in the near to intermediate term. Although the transition away from conventional petroleum poses some short-term adjustment problems, supplies of alternative fuels and nonfuel resources are adequate regardless of population growth. As any particular resource becomes physically scarce, its concomitant price rise stimulates conservation, improvements in extraction technology, and the search for less expensive substitutes. These adaptations serve to greatly mute, and perhaps entirely counteract, any negative effect of resource depletion on the standard of living.

In theory, the price mechanism provides an effective means of coping with the allocation of scarce resources so long as the structure of markets is, technically speaking, complete: that is, there are enough markets to trade resources—exhaustible and renewable—over the indefinite future and to share risks. However, a complete set of markets does not exist, even in developed countries, and in developing countries, as we discussed above, the markets that do function have many distortions, impairing their ability to allocate resources optimally over time. Consequently, population growth may be more directly linked to inefficient resource use in reality than in theory, although population policies appear to be a very crude instrument for dealing with inefficient markets. But since it is neither simple nor costless to remove distortions or to create markets where none exist, the prescription of letting markets function efficiently without worrying about resource exhaustion must be qualified.

Thus it is not clear that the effective price of resources will rise over time or that slower population growth will delay the date at which an ascending price level reaches any given point. Even if slower population growth did defer the date of any given stage of resource depletion, it does not follow that it would increase the number of people who had enjoyed low resource prices. It is more likely that slower population growth would simply stretch a more-or-less fixed queue of resource users more thinly over time. While this could, in principle, provide more time for serendipitous technological advances in resource extraction or substitution, we do not find this an important factor relative to price-driven technological change.

On balance, then, we find that concern about the impact of rapid population growth on resource exhaustion has often been exaggerated, and, in any case, that the effect of changes in population growth in developing countries on global resource use has been and will probably continue to be quite weak.

2

Will slower population growth increase the growth rate of per capita income through increasing per capita availability of renewable resources?

In contrast to exhaustible resources, biotic resources like forests, fisheries, and agricultural land can be renewed by natural processes. Renewable resources are potentially capable of providing economic services in perpetuity so long as their regenerative capability is not damaged. Consequently, they pose a different set of issues than those for exhaustible resources.

There are two mechanisms that can create a link between population size or growth rates and the availability of renewable resources. One can be termed the issue of diminishing returns. When a population is larger, a member of the population will have, on average, fewer of the renewable resources to use in production and consumption. Certain important resources—oxygen, for example–are so abundant that greater numbers of people have no material effect on the amount available per person. But others, such as arable land, are sufficiently limited in abundance that their diminishing availability per person can reduce labor productivity and restrain per capita production and consumption possibilities. Unlike the case of exhaustible resources, the number of persons alive at a moment of time can have an enduring effect on each person's available resources. In a steady-state world population of 10 billion, for example, each member will have less arable land per capita than in a steady-state population of 5 billion. This difference will persist through time and over individuals born into the two populations.

The second issue is one of resource depletion. The natural processes that produce resource renewal do not operate automatically. They are subject to human interference and disruption as well as to the vagaries of nature. This fact becomes even more salient when effective property rights governing access to the resource do not exist or are not enforced. Resources that are not governed by well-defined access rules are called common-property resources. Because no private or public sector agent controls the disposition of the stock, users of the resource must pay only the cost of harvesting it. Because the price is lower than it would be if the asset value of the stock were taken into account, the resource will be over-exploited, and there will be inadequate incentives for resource conservation.

Certainly the most important renewable resource in most developing countries is arable land. There are, however, other important renewable resources subject to depletion, many of them common-property resources. Access to vast extents of forest in some of these countries is virtually unrestricted, and deforestation due to commercial lumbering, fuelwood gathering, and agriculture is now a major issue. Similarly, fishing is an important worldwide source of food, but overfishing has reduced yields in many ocean areas. Freshwater is another important renewable resource, particularly due to its use for irrigation. Although the economic relationships in each of these cases are complex, population size and growth play at least some role in the demand for these resources.

DIMINISHING RETURNS TO LABOR IN AGRICULTURE

Historical Responses to Diminishing Returns

The relations between population and agricultural production are played out against a backdrop of static diminishing marginal returns to labor. Diminishing returns to labor were evident in Europe over a long stretch of time in which productive techniques were changing very slowly. Time series of real wage and population figures for England, France, and a composite of countries between 1300 and 1750 leave little doubt that exogenous changes in population, induced by epidemics, plagues, and weather changes, affected average wages: periods of unusually small population numbers had unusually high wages (Lee, 1980; Gould, 1972; Slicher van Bath, 1963).

One reason these relations are not very evident in contemporary populations is that many factors besides land and labor have come to play an important role in agricultural production. The application of fertilizer, irrigation, and a great variety of biological techniques (new seeds, new methods of crop rotation, leguminous crops) have loosened the link between labor productivity in agriculture and the land/labor ratio. However, these new factors are themselves often subject to diminishing returns. There is evidence that output gains from added fertilizer use in the United States (Crosson, 1982) and in a cross-section of developing countries (Brown, 1984) are less than they were when fertilizer was less intensively used. Likewise, output gains from irrigation encounter diminishing returns from waterlogging and increased salinity of the land (Brown, 1981; Hayami and Ruttan, 1984; Hinman, 1984). But the existence of diminishing returns to these factors does not necessarily pose economic barriers to their increased use. Indeed, the combination of increasing fertilizer use and diminishing returns to it in industrial countries is a natural response to a long-term decline in the real price of fertilizer. Such diminishing returns also can be and have been to some extent offset by changes in plant varieties and production methods.

A second reason that declining labor productivity in agriculture resulting from land scarcity has not been widely observed in developing countries is that massive additions to the stock of land under cultivation have occurred during this century. Most of the gains in food production between 1900 and 1950 were a result of expanding the area under cultivation (Brown, 1981; Johnson, 1974). Contrary to Ricardian assumptions, this added land was not necessarily of inferior quality; it may simply have been located further from existing settlements (Ghatak and Ingersent, 1984). Since 1950, however, most of the output gains have resulted from increased yields per unit of cultivated area. For example, it is estimated that increased yields contributed 62 percent of the gain in world agricultural production in the 1960s and 1970s (Mellor and Johnston, 1984). There are still substantial possibilities, however, for expanding the amount of land under cultivation in parts of Africa and Latin America.

The net result of increases in land under cultivation, increased use of fertilizer and irrigation, and improved agricultural techniques is that the growth rate of total agricultural production on a worldwide basis and for developing countries as a whole–except for parts of Africa–has consistently exceeded population growth rates in the past two decades (Food and Agriculture Organization, 1981). The real prices of the major sources of calories for people in poor nations have declined in recent decades, and the proportion of the labor force in agriculture in developing countries with market economies declined from 68 percent in 1965 to 58 percent in 1981 (Johnson, 1985).

Africa represents an important exception to rising per capita agricultural production. Per capita agricultural output in Africa fell by an average of 1 percent per year between the early 1960s and 1980 (Food and Agriculture Organization, 1981:22). However, Africa has a relatively high ratio of arable land to population, which suggests that the decline in per capita agricultural output reflects factors other than diminishing returns due to population growth. These factors reflect a host of human and institutional barriers to expanded output, including a very weak human resource base for agricultural research, extension, and entrepreneurship; overvalued foreign exchange rates that discourage domestic production; high taxes on both food crops and export crops; an urban bias in development strategies and investment; and failed experiments in agrarian socialism (Eicher, 1984; Economic Commission for Africa, 1984). Eicher (1984) argues that many of these conditions are a legacy of colonialism and that others have been encouraged by foreign advisers. It seems reasonable to expect that in combination with these conditions, faster population growth will aggravate problems of low labor productivity in agriculture in Africa (Binswanger and Pingali, 1984).

There are many countries that have successfully increased their agricultural output despite the problem of diminishing returns. Perhaps the best documented case is Japan, which in 1880 had only 5 percent as much arable land per worker as did the United States. Yet total agricultural production in both countries grew at an average annual rate of 1.6 percent during the next 100 years (Hayami and Ruttan, 1985b). The Japanese solution to its high labor/land ratio was to develop and use more labor-intensive methods of production than countries like the United States, to rely heavily on irrigation, and to introduce biological techniques to increase yields (Pingali and Binswanger, 1984; Hayami and Ruttan, 1985b). The Japanese-type solution has characterized many other areas in Asia, including Taiwan, Java, South Korea, the central plains of Thailand, the Punjab, and the Philippines (Pingali and Binswanger, 1984; Hayami and Ruttan, 1985b; Muscat, 1984; Khan, 1984).

While there are many examples of successful adaptations to high labor/land ratios, there are other examples where intensification of agriculture has apparently led to reduced labor productivity, sometimes accompanied by soil depletion, exhaustion, and even abandonment. For example, the Mayan civilization may have expanded its population beyond the point that could be permanently sustained given its land and technical endowments (Deevey et al., 1979). Much of northern Africa might have lost its agricultural potential from a combination of climatic change and population pressure (Kirchner et al., 1984). More contemporary examples of such processes have been noted in Zambia (Allan, 1965) and the inter-Andine region of Ecuador (Gourou, 1980). Gourou (1980:73-74) also cites the Kamba in Kenya, the Sukumas in Tanzania, and the Jabros in Sudan as groups forced to migrate to other areas because of degraded soil produced by overgrazing. Beckford (1984) argues in more general terms that institutional structures in developing countries create rigidities that prevent or inhibit the kind of adaptive responses to population pressure and market opportunities exhibited in Japan.

Perhaps the most important contemporary country demonstrating diminishing returns to labor in agriculture is Bangladesh. According to Khan (1984), real agricultural wages in Bangladesh in the 1970s were below what they had been in the 1830s. Much of the decline occurred in the period of most rapid population growth after 1950. The decline in real wages was accompanied by an apparent increase in landlessness from an estimated 7.3 percent of the farm labor force in 1951 to 26.1 percent in 1977 (see Cain, 1983, for a skeptical view on the quality of these data); a decline in average caloric consumption per capita; and a rise in the proportion of the population living in poverty. Khan can find no other explanation for these disturbing trends than the rapid increase in population combined with institutional rigidities. Ghatak and Ingersent (1984) raise the question of whether it is realistic to speak of possibilities for adopting new technologies in response to population pressure in countries like Bangladesh, where labor is already extremely intensively used. The population-push model of technical change in agriculture initially proposed by Boserup (1965) may have no technological stages left to offer a country in which agrarian density is already very high. Surely there are many possibilities for improving agricultural output in Bangladesh, but additional density of population does not appear necessary to induce their adoption. Clearly, one must examine carefully the preconditions for intensified agriculture in a specific country before reaching a verdict on the long-term effects of population growth on its labor productivity in agriculture.

Future Prospects for Agricultural Intensification

It is important to note that many soils in tropical areas do not have the same capacity for intensified production as soils in temperate areas. Tropical soils are usually deficient in important minerals, such as phosphorus and nitrogen, and because they are poor in humus they have a reduced capacity to adsorb fertilizer. The low adsorptive capacity of many tropical clays, in combination with heavy rainfall, results in rapid leaching of important minerals from the soil. And since organic matter generally decomposes more rapidly in tropical areas, manure remains active a much shorter time than in temperate areas (Gourou, 1980). In arid and semiarid lands, the rainfall required to support a dense population is lacking, although phosphorus can be introduced to increase the soil's capacity to adsorb water (Breman and de Wit, 1983).

Despite their natural disadvantages, some tropical lands are very intensively farmed, and a great deal of additional intensification is possible. Certain schemes in the Amazon have resulted in continuous farming at high yields (Sedjo and Clawson, 1984). In some countries a variety of soil types exist, and a rise in the population/land ratio can move cultivation away from midslope areas, where potential productivity per unit of land is relatively low but where less land preparation is required, to lower-lying areas where potential land productivity is higher (Pingali and Binswanger, 1985). Such a movement typically incurs an expense in the form of a reduction in leisure hours, which are often relatively high among nomadic farmers and in lightly farmed areas (Gourou, 1980:Chapter 7). Because of this relationship, many low-lying areas in sparsely populated parts of Africa are uncultivated, although they could support intensive rice production with other inputs as well as increased labor.

To gain a sense of agricultural production possibilities under alternative techniques, the U.N. Food and Agriculture Organization (FAO) and the International Institute for Applied Systems Analysis (IIASA) undertook a study of the number of people who could be supported by the agricultural production of specific areas in the developing world. The world was divided into tens of thousands of small regions distinguished by soil type and climate. All potentially cultivable land was assumed to be used for food crops, except for 0.05 hectares per person devoted to all other uses. Production potential was evaluated under three assumed levels of input: a low level, corresponding to traditional farming practices in developing countries (manual labor, hand tools, and the current mixture of crops); a high level, assuming the optimal mixture of crops for a particular area and substantial mechanization; and an intermediate level that is roughly an average of the other two (Food and Agriculture Organization, 1983). The high level of inputs, though technologically feasible, is very often well beyond what is economically feasible.

Under the low level of inputs, 54 countries were identified as "critical" in 1975, having insufficient food production capacity to support their current population. Under the high-input level, the figure was 13. The numbers of countries grow to 64 (of which 10 are in the Middle East–see below) and 19, respectively, under the projected national populations of 2000. Most of the critical countries are below average in size, although India appears on the list in 1975 under the low-input level; with high inputs, India could support 2.5 times its expected population in 2000. Zaire has enormous agricultural potential by this calculation, able to support 62 times its expected 2000 population of 46 million with high inputs–enough to feed the entire population of Africa several times over–and 6 times its expected population even under low inputs. The 24 largest developing countries as a whole (excluding China) are projected to be able to support a total of 21.9 billion persons under high inputs by the year 2000, more than seven times their projected populations. As discussed above, these figures constitute technological upper limits that help to frame discussion, but they do not constitute realistic targets.

The economic possibilities for food production may, in fact, be far below the technical limits, since food will be produced only if it is in the economic interests of farmers to do so. Srinivasan (1985) reviews a number of elaborate simulation studies that seek to incorporate economic processes in food production forecasts. These studies–notably one by the Food and Agriculture Organization (1981), *Global 2000* (Council on Environmental Quality and U.S. Department of State, 1980), and the IIASA system of models (Srinivasan, 1985)–differ in sophistication, but they are roughly consistent in forecasting small gains in average per capita caloric intake by 2000. The IIASA model, for instance, projects an 11 percent total gain in per capita caloric intake in developing countries over the period 1980-2000. The FAO and *Global 2000* reports stress that large investments in agriculture will be necessary to achieve gains of this magnitude. Moreover, the Food and Agriculture Organization (1981) projects that 260 million to 390 million people will still be severely undernourished in 2000 despite the gains in average intake. Srinivasan (1985) surmises that all the models may be somewhat pessimistic because they are unable to model the constructive responses of investment, population, technology, and institutions to changing agricultural conditions. But he also notes that a failure of institutions to respond to population growth could result in a decrease in access to food by the poor due to an increase in landlessness and the fragmentation of already small landholdings into even smaller parcels that cannot support even one family.

Unlike the model of the Food and Agriculture Organization (1983), the three economic models cited above stress the importance of international trade. A country whose agricultural production falls below its population's needs for food is in critical shape only if it does not trade with other nations to satisfy its needs for food. The fact that many oil-exporting Middle Eastern countries appear on the critical list makes clear the arbitrariness of a standard of self-sufficiency. Indeed, many more people would be counted as living in critical countries merely by arbitrarily dividing the world into smaller and smaller nations. The importance of trade in the world food equation has grown considerably with improvements in bulk transportation and in the political climate. Imports of food rose from 1.5 to 5 percent of production in developing countries between the mid-1950s and the mid-1970s (Mellor and Johnston, 1984). The United States increased its cereal exports from 37 million tons per year in the early 1960s to 115 million tons in 1981. Some analysts view with alarm the increasing imports of food in developing countries and their increased dependence on American exports (Brown, 1981). But some of the growth is a result of higher incomes combined with the comparative advantage of the United States in food production. Taiwan, for example, used less than 1 percent of its cereals for animal feeding in 1961, but because of rising incomes it used 60 percent of its cereals in this fashion in 1981, importing a substantial fraction of its "needs" (Mellor and Johnston, 1984). Another part of the increase in world food trade is a result of improvements in transportation and storage that allow nations to make better use of their comparative advantages in production. One would expect greater specialization and more trade as integration of nations into a world economy proceeds. Food is unique, however, in its ability to sustain life, and the increasing dependence of the rest of the world on North American exports must be viewed in this light.

When transportation is available, agricultural areas in developing countries already have an incentive to intensify production and to increase yields even in the absence of population pressure. There are many examples of agricultural production in developing countries responding to market opportunities. The building of railroads in Africa has typically led to intensified production techniques near railroad lines. Conversely, deteriorating transportation systems in Zaire have prevented high prices on the border from stimulating production in the interior (Pingali and Binswanger, 1984). The more intensive farming methods commonly observed near urban areas in developing countries attest to the importance of markets in the choice of technique (Gourou, 1980:Chapter 9).

If markets provide incentives to intensify agricultural production even in the absence of population growth, the question is what additional role, if any, is played by population growth. The answer is that population growth can both create markets and increase the demand within particular markets. Agricultural goods are relatively bulky, with a high weight and volume per unit value. Many are also subject to rapid spoilage. Consequently, a higher fraction of production is directed toward nearby markets than is the case for such goods as textiles. The size of local markets for food is therefore more important than it is for many goods, particularly when transportation facilities are poor. Population growth can also increase incentives for and reduce per capita costs of improvement in transportation facilities and thereby create access to new markets—one of the most important potential benefits of growth—although not much is known about the ranges of density over which this might matter (Simon, 1981). Clearly, then, population growth in local areas can stimulate agricultural production.

However, the fact that population growth can stimulate agricultural production does not mean that it automatically will. No response that requires human institutional and organizational adaptation is automatic. Northern Brazil, Argentina, and Uruguay have been cited as areas in which policies that are affected by biases in the distribution of political and economic resources have prevented appropriate responses to changing conditions (de Janvry, 1984). Indeed, the literature is rife with examples of poor organization of agriculture, including improper techniques, poorly chosen crops, inadequate labor input, and government interventions that prevent proper price signals from being transmitted to producers (Bale and Duncan, 1983). Depending on the circumstances, population growth can exacerbate these problems or provide the stimulus needed to solve them. Whether the very large potential for expanded world agricultural output will be realized depends fundamentally on whether agricultural research efforts will be sufficient; whether markets for agricultural output will be allowed to function effectively; and whether other social institutions, credit markets, educational systems, labor markets, and government investment priorities are supportive. As noted above, some of these conditions are affected by population growth itself. Rosenzweig et al. (1984) elaborate on this theme, noting how labor markets can be expected to change as agrarian density increases and how the evolution of property rights induced by population pressure can be expected to improve credit markets.

The importance of agricultural research attuned to local conditions, with appropriate extension activities, has been repeatedly emphasized. The scope for research is great: for example, only a tiny fraction of all plant and animal species have been domesticated to play a role in the human food system (Revelle, 1976). Of the 350,000 plant species identified by botanists, only 3,000 or so have been tried as sources of food or other useful materials. The rate of return from investment in agricultural research and extension activities has often been calculated to be extremely high. Evenson (1984a) compiles estimates of internal rates of return to agricultural research, about half of which pertain to developing countries; only 4 of the 62 studies show annual rates of return below 20 percent. Many authorities have stressed the importance of adapting research to local conditions and integrating extension activities into that research (e.g., Eicher and Staatz, 1984).

Because of characteristics of agriculture, governments in general have a major role to play in agricultural research, particularly in the area of biological techniques. Some people have argued that farmer-generated technical changes do not appear capable of proceeding rapidly enough to keep pace with population growth (Pingali and Binswanger, 1984). Furthermore, the benefits from research in genetics and soil science cannot all be captured by private firms, since nothing prevents technical information and most seed varieties from spreading from farmer to farmer. These characteristics suggest that the private sector will underinvest in agricultural research. In addition, much of the benefit of agricultural research goes to consumers rather than producers because of low price elasticity of demand for agricultural products (Ruttan and Hayami, 1984a).

Semiarid lands, because of their fertile soils, long growing seasons, and low humidity that reduces crop diseases, are particularly promising areas for expanded production (Hinman, 1984). The potential role of research in expanding production also appears great in tropical Africa, where there has been little experience with intensified farming techniques, although some are now being introduced from Asia. Intensive rice cultivation can be done in low-lying areas that are often unused, and the cultivation of fruit trees also has much potential (Binswanger and Pingali, 1984; Gourou, 1980). Unfortunately, tropical Africa is also where the human resources needed for agricultural research and extension activities are least abundant (Eicher, 1984).

Research and extension activities alone are not sufficient for major advances in production. Many institutional changes involving land tenure systems, credit markets, and markets for inputs and outputs will be required. Hayami and Ruttan (1985b) find evidence that changes in the availability of labor relative to land have created demands for institutional reform, pointing in particular toward experience in Japan, the United States, and the Punjab. Others have cited the enclosure movement and other institutional changes in Europe in the seventeenth and eighteenth centuries as a response to population growth (North and Thomas, 1973). But Hayami and Ruttan (1984:32) stress that "growing poverty and inequality will be an almost certain result if efforts to generate technical progress are insufficient to overcome the decreasing return to labor due to growing population pressure on land."

One recent study in north India attempts to pull together evidence on the effect of agricultural population density on agricultural production in the area, including the responses that work through many of the factors considered above: research efforts, provision of credit, electrification, roads, irrigation, and intensity of land use (Evenson, 1984b). It concludes that population density has a significantly positive effect on the intensity of irrigation and on the net cultivated area but that it has a negative impact on research investment, road expenditure, electrification, and credit. The net effect is that a 10 percent expansion in population density is associated with a 6.7 percent increase in output. In other words, output per capita falls 3.3 percent for a 10 percent expansion in population. The poorest groups suffer the largest decline in real income when density increases, while rents paid to owners of land increase sharply. These results imply that a drop in population density of 10 percent would raise the real incomes of the landless by 6.4 percent. Before allowance for the indirect effects of density, the gain in incomes for the landless would have been 14.7 percent. Lee's (1980) estimates for preindustrial England show similar effects: a 10 percent increase in population size depressed real wages by 22 percent and raised rents by 19 percent. Evenson's (1984b) results are tentative because population density could be in part responding to the availability of infrastructural investments, in which case the impact of density on output is likely to be overstated. If so, the loss in per capita income resulting from population growth would be larger than indicated.

In a related cross-sectional study of agricultural production in 52 specific locations around the world, Pingali and Binswanger (1985) find that increases in the amount of labor applied per unit of land are associated with greater intensification of agricultural production (i.e., more frequent plantings), which is, in turn, hypothesized to be a response to population pressure. More frequent planting–controlling other inputs such as capital investment in land and the use of tractors and animal power–is associated with slightly lower output per hour of labor spent on cultivation. The authors speculate that the effect would have been larger had it been possible to control for the amount of labor time used in land preparation, which is expected to increase with intensification of agriculture. The analysis does not fully allow for the farmer's role in choosing intensification or technique as a response to population pressure. However, these results are in the same direction as those of Evenson and Lee, suggesting that slower population growth will increase the growth rate of labor productivity in agriculture.

DEGRADATION AND ENHANCEMENT OF AGRICULTURAL RESOURCES

By stimulating an intensification of agriculture through shortened fallow time, multiple plantings, more use of fertilizer or irrigation, better weed and pest control, and the like, population growth can change the quality of land used in production. Some of the changes reduce land productivity. Erosion of topsoil can accelerate when production is intensified unless proper conservation measures are taken. Shortening the fallow time will usually reduce soil fertility because there will be less natural growth on the land to supply nutrients to the soil. But intensification can also improve soil productivity, especially in swampy areas (Pingali and Binswanger, 1985). Operations to clear land of trees and stumps obviously represent one-time investments, sometimes induced by population growth, that can make subsequent tillage easier. Other investments in land improvement may also require a certain minimum density before they become profitable. For example, Pingali and Binswanger (1984) suggest that the failure of large-scale irrigation schemes in sub-Saharan Africa can be attributed to the sparseness of population and a corresponding lack of demand for extending the cultivated area.

If market mechanisms are working properly, landowners or public sector managers will resist the degradation of their land, or encourage its enhancement, so as to maximize its long-term asset value. In this matter investments in land productivity do not differ from other forms of investment that increase future production capacity. If more rapid population growth is seen as extending into the future, landowners will have added incentives to invest in their land because the future market will be larger relative to the present one; but the supply of funds for investment may be reduced because more rapid growth increases current consumption demands. The effect on the volume of investment in land conservation efforts cannot be predicted a priori, and we know of no careful empirical studies on this matter. Impressions of informed observers are widely disparate: Pingali and Binswanger (1984:12) argue that "anti-erosion investments in land are becoming increasingly common in the more recently intensified areas of Africa"; Brown (1981:995) argues that "in their efforts to keep up with the doubling of world food demand since mid-century, many of the world's farmers have adopted agricultural production practices that are leading to excessive rates of soil erosion." In a later article, Brown (1984) cites China, Nepal, Indonesia, Venezuela, Ethiopia, Pakistan, and Andean countries as areas where population pressure is resulting in excessive rates of soil erosion. Smil (1984) provides a vivid account of rapid soil degradation in China between 1950 and 1980 as a result of poor cropping practices, improper land reclamation, careless irrigation, and deforestation. A recent review of data on the extent of erosion in developing countries concludes that the data are sparse in quantity and uncertain in quality (Crosson, 1983).

It should be noted that what is an excessive rate of soil erosion to one observer may correspond to efficient use of land over time. It may seem curious that any rate of erosion could be efficient, but in fact the aggregate of private and social decisions that establish the market rate of interest discount future consumption relative to present consumption. In discussions of market solutions to issues of resource scarcity, it is useful to recognize that markets will serve only to reflect the desires of groups that can express their preferences (Smith and Krutilla, 1979). Because future generations may not be well represented in these markets, some observers feel that government investment decisions should adopt lower discount rates than the private market; others suggest that people in the future are likely to be wealthier than at present, so that such interventions would exacerbate intertemporal income inequalities; still others argue that elected governments cannot be relied on to use below-market discount rates since their incentives are to emphasize short-term goals determined by political expediency. The issues related to investment in soil conservation are no different in principle from those related to other forms of investment, although there is often a different psychological connotation when conditions are actually getting worse instead of not improving as fast as they could be. Governments can choose to impose different discount rates in different markets, and in the United States, government policy regarding soil conservation has not, in fact, relied exclusively on market mechanisms but has actively promoted a variety of erosion control programs, the latest of which is "conservation tillage" (Crosson, 1982). But in India, the political support for soil conservation programs may be minuscule (Brown, 1981).

Whatever the situation for privately owned land, it is widely agreed that land as a common-property resource will usually be degraded too rapidly relative to the rate that would be established through a market. The reason is simply that those people who contemplate making investments in conservation will not reap the full benefits of those investments and therefore will underinvest. Optimal levels of conservation can be established if all the users of the common-property resource can agree to make production and investment decisions as a group; as a group, they can capture all the benefits of conservation investments.

There is very little information on the degree to which land is held in common in various parts of the world or the degree to which common lands are group administered (Crosson, 1983). The absence of land-ownership rights is very likely most frequent in sub-Saharan Africa, where land is most abundant relative to labor. However, much of the land is tribally administered. Eicher (1984:455) characterizes land tenure in Africa as a "communal tenure system of public ownership and private use rights of land." Africa is a particularly vulnerable continent to land degradation, since much of it consists of tropical soils with few nutrients except those contained in the plants that grow on it (Gourou, 1980). Much of Africa's land surface is still farmed with shifting cultivation under the fallow system (Pingali and Binswanger, 1984). It is well known and widely observed that shortened fallow time will reduce the amount of nutrients returned to the soil for use in any particular crop cycle. In turn, a shortage of nutrients will reduce soil's water absorption capacity.

It is reasonable to expect that, as populations grow, the demand for establishing property rights to land will increase, as it did in Europe (North and Thomas, 1973). Hayami and Ruttan (1985a) review the evolution of property rights to agricultural land in Japan, Thailand, and a Philippine village, finding that population growth was instrumental in the process, although new production techniques and expanded possibilities for trade also played a role. Binswanger and Pingali (1984) show that sparsely populated areas of Africa generally have easy access to land, with the transition from shifting to permanent cultivation associated with a parallel movement toward privatization of agricultural land. But land tenure systems are not always smoothly accommodating. The Economic Commission for Africa (1984) notes that efforts to change such systems in Burundi, Comoros, and Zaire have met with considerable resistance on the part of individual farmers and tribal groups. By fostering the evolution of property rights that are conducive to conservation, population growth is likely to result eventually in better land protection as institutions adapt. In the meantime, however, it is possible that rapid population growth will exacerbate the tendency for a too rapid rate of land degradation on common lands.

Other factors unrelated to population growth can also produce a deterioration in land quality. As noted above, improved markets will provide incentives to intensify production regardless of population density. Higher incomes in developing countries will increase demand for agricultural products. Social groups can be forced onto marginal and more readily degradable land by more powerful groups without any necessary demographic propellant. Ignorance about proper soil conservation practices can produce rapid degradation even in the face of a strong desire to conserve. Such lack of knowledge is particularly threatening in an "industry"–agriculture–that is atomistically organized. Writing about U.S. farmers in 1984–surely among the world's most knowledgeable–Crosson (1984) argues that farmers' knowledge of relations between intensity of production and erosion is based primarily on their experience with their own land and that extrapolations of their own experience may be a poor guide to predicting future effects of intensified production.

FORESTS AND FISHERIES

There is increasing evidence of loss of forest reserves, although the author of one of the major survey efforts commissioned by the National Academy of Sciences (Myers, 1980) appears to have reduced dramatically his estimate of the rate of permanent conversion of tropical forests since the Academy report (Postel, 1984). A survey by the FAO produced rates of deforestation of tropical forests that, if continued, would shrink the size of such forests by 10-15 percent by 2000 (Postel, 1984). Shifting cultivation accounts for about 45 percent of all forest clearing and for about 70 percent in Africa. Examples of landless persons encroaching on forests to establish shifting or permanent cultivation have been cited in Peru, Thailand, India, and the Philippines (Postel, 1984). Myers (1980) concluded that an increasing intensity of agricultural practice resulting from population pressure was the leading cause of the conversion of tropical moist forests to other uses. A direct link between population pressure and deforestation has been created by government policy in Indonesia, where a "transmigration scheme" has attempted to move the population from the most densely populated agricultural areas to forested areas (Sedjo and Clawson, 1984:138).

In developing countries, three-quarters of the wood that is harvested from forests is used for fuel (Postel, 1984). The declining abundance of forests in certain areas has produced a fuel shortage of major proportions. In Gambia and Central Tanzania, firewood has become so scarce that the average household requires 250-300 worker-days to meet its annual fuelwood needs (Kirchner et al., 1984). In many Central American and West African cities, a typical family spends one-quarter of its budget on fuelwood and charcoal (Postel, 1984). Large price increases for fuelwood have recently been noted in the Cameroon; Bombay, India; and the Ivory Coast (Postel, 1984). The shortage of fuelwood in some areas is limiting the possibilities for agriculture. In Burkina Faso, there is considerable potential for soybean cultivation, but it is reported that the shortage of firewood required in food preparation has helped prevent this potential from being realized (Kirchner et al., 1984).

While an important aspect of fuelwood deforestation is linked to population pressure, it must be noted that low incomes are a more direct cause of the problem. Wood is a relatively inefficient source of energy for cooking and heating, and it is bulky and difficult to transport. Slightly more expensive substitutes such as kerosene are, in contrast, both more efficient and easier to use, and seem to be preferred to wood when affordable (MacKellar and Vining, 1985). Should depletion significantly raise the price of fuelwood relative to alternatives, or should incomes increase, the link between population growth and deforestation due to the demand for fuelwood would be significantly weakened.

Forests are important not only for their direct products but also for housing millions of species, for preventing soil erosion, and for their aesthetic value. Smil (1984) reports that massive deforestation in China has accelerated erosion and produced worsening droughts and floods. Contributing to rapid forest depletion is the fact that forests have been essentially freely accessible to potential users in many parts of the developing world, so that overrapid rates of exploitation can be expected. Sedjo and Clawson (1984) argue that the regions of the world where deforestation is not a serious problem are precisely those where the common-property problem has been dealt with satisfactorily. The accessibility of forests in developing countries results from both the difficulties of limiting access and the relatively low value of forest resources. This low value is reflected in the continuation of slash-and-burn agricultural practices in many areas, especially Africa (Gourou, 1980; Myers, 1980). In such areas, the value of wood is not sufficiently large to make it economically worthwhile to harvest the wood for sale, and the lumber value of the resource literally goes up in smoke. In fact, the harvesting of fuelwoods from tropical forests is said to be only a marginal factor in the conversion of these woods to nonforest uses (Myers, 1980). Much of the firewood is obtained from savannah woodlands, scrub and brush patches, and local woodlots.

At the opposite end of the spectrum, there are clear rules for access to commercial forests in the United States. Such forests occupy one-quarter of the U.S. land area, and another one-eighth consists of forested areas administered by governments. As a whole, the trend in annual wood growth per acre in the United States has been upward since 1952 (Clawson, 1982); that is, forests are accumulating more wood than is being harvested annually. Puerto Rico is another example of successful forest management. After being 90 percent deforested, much of the loss has been reversed. Such management is not out of the reach of many developing countries. The growth of "plantation forests" in Latin America is fast enough that they are expected to account for half of the region's industrial wood production by the year 2000 (Sedjo and Clawson, 1984:152).

Ocean fisheries are the classic illustration of problems related to common-property resources (Dasgupta and Heal, 1979). Because access to the stock of fish is difficult to regulate when fisheries extend beyond a single political jurisdiction, overfishing may reduce the fish population so much that yields fall. In extreme cases, overfishing may even reduce the stock beneath the level required for the population to maintain itself. If this occurs, the stock may all but disappear, and the fishery may cease to be commercially viable. For example, the disappearance of the Peruvian anchovy fisheries in 1972 has been attributed to overfishing (Clark, 1978).

Because most important commercial fisheries extend beyond the 200-mile economic exploitation zone for a single nation, no jurisdiction is able to regulate catch sizes, and catches currently exceed the levels recommended by international fishing bodies. As a consequence, world fish yields on a per capita basis have ceased growing, and prices have increased fairly sharply (MacKellar and Vining, 1985). Fish is an important food source, representing 25 percent of world animal protein consumption, and it is also an important source of animal feed. Given the difficulties in establishing international policies limiting catches, rapid population growth in the developing countries, through its effect on world food demand, is likely to contribute to the continued overexploitation of the world's fisheries.

CONCLUSIONS

Rapid population growth poses two problems for agriculture. First, if no other conditions of production change, expansion of the agricultural labor force probably reduces labor productivity and correspondingly lowers agricultural wages. Second, population growth can accelerate the degradation of renewable resources. Although many other forces are capable of producing erosion, population growth can do so by expanding the amount of land under cultivation and intensifying land use, especially where property rights are ill-defined and where there is substantial ignorance about good agricultural practices. Similarly, there is evidence that forests and fisheries are being overexploited and that the real prices of lumber and fish have increased. Because demand for fuelwood, forest land, and fish are all sensitive to population, continued rapid population growth poses a risk to these resources.

The extent to which slower population growth would alleviate these problems depends on the degree to which the problems lead to other solutions through institutional and technological adaptation. With regard to diminishing returns to labor, the growth of population can induce a wide variety of changes in agricultural production techniques. Experience in several countries suggests that such induced innovations can offset much of the initially negative impact of population growth on labor productivity. The responses include intensified cropping practices; introduction of additional factors of production, such as fertilizer and irrigation; improved markets; and expanded research efforts. It is worthwhile noting that, with the important exception of Africa, per capita agricultural output has risen in most developing regions during the recent period of rapid population growth. Similarly, population growth can encourage changes in property rights that boost incentives for soil conservation. Management techniques that conserve forests and fisheries are known, and continued price increases will strengthen incentives for using them.

However, adaptive responses to population growth are not automatic: they are constrained by natural conditions, such as the limited responsiveness of many tropical soils to intensification, and conditioned by human institutions. Among the most important of these institutions are rights governing access to renewable resources, markets to transmit signals of scarcity, and government policies that affect the agricultural infrastructure and research. Furthermore, the institutional change and other adaptive responses that are necessary will have to be unusually rapid in developing countries relative to Western historical experience simply because population growth rates are more rapid. Institutional adaptation may be particularly difficult in the case of forests and fisheries because some kind of negotiated collective action is necessary to resolve the common-property aspects of the problem. In short, if institutions do not adapt as rapidly as needed, slower population growth can retard the decline of labor productivity and the degradation of common resources. Of course, the most direct policy prescription is to fix the institutions. But fixing existing institutions, or establishing new ones, may be difficult, especially where there are severe and long-standing political inadequacies, as may be the case in Africa, or where there are fundamental technical problems in restricting access to a resource.

Finally, it should be noted that this chapter addresses aggregate agricultural production, not distribution; that is the subject of Question 7. Perfectly functioning markets are no guarantee against starvation when there are extreme disparities of wealth.

3

Will slower population growth alleviate pollution and the degradation of the natural environment?

The quality of the natural environment, including air and water, climatic conditions, and the number and abundance of species of plants and animals, has direct significance for the health, economic production, and aesthetics of human populations. In addition to being essential requirements for human life, air and water are direct inputs into many production processes and also provide an important economic service by absorbing the residuals of production processes (Smith and Krutilla, 1979). Climatic conditions, of course, represent an important parameter in agricultural production. Climate combines with plant and animal species to create aesthetically appealing environments that can be a basis for tourism. And naturally occurring plant and animal species represent sources of genetic diversity that may be important in developing new products through biotechnology (Miller et al., 1986).

Production and consumption of industrial goods provide the primary link between population and environmental degradation, so the strength of the linkage may depend importantly on income levels. However, there are many processes of environmental degradation that depend more directly on population. For example, while most of the buildup of atmospheric carbon dioxide responsible for the emerging "greenhouse" effect is due to fossil fuel combustion, predominantly in the developed countries, some 23 to 43 percent is due to the burning of forests, primarily for land clearance, in developing countries (Woodwell et al., 1983), which may well be linked to population increase. But because only a moderate proportion of the addition to atmospheric carbon dioxide is attributable to activities in developing countries

35

and because the sensitivity of this addition to changes in population size or growth is uncertain, the effect of population trends in developing countries on the carbon dioxide problem may be minor.

Environmental resources are mostly renewable, but as with other renewable resources, human action can interfere with the renewal process in ways that produce permanent degradation. This possibility is most evident in the case of total species extinction, which is clearly an irreversible process. The atmospheric buildup of carbon dioxide and fluorocarbons as by-products of production has effects that are also so long term as to mimic irreversibility, as are effects of siltation of major water resources. Eutrophication of lakes and effects of acid rain are processes that can be reversed, but probably not in less than a generation.

Reflecting their physical characteristics and seeming abundance, environmental resources typically have no property rights that govern access to them. Because of this common-property aspect, many of these resources tend to be overexploited. For instance, when access to air and water is unregulated, polluters can impose substantial costs on other users, and in many cases, these costs are greater than the costs of pollution abatement. Thus, there would be a net gain to society if there were some institution–such as pollution taxes or a market in pollution rights–that would allocate rights to the resource so as to balance costs and benefits. However, there are a number of barriers to setting up such institutions.

It is both analytically and empirically difficult to determine the optimum levels of pollution taxes or to specify the conditions required for efficient markets in pollution rights. The use of either pollution taxes or markets in pollution rights has had relatively few applications (Starrett, 1972). On a pragmatic level, imposing and enforcing new property rights to previously unpriced resources is politically and administratively difficult. Vested interests that would suffer losses from the new assignment of property rights may oppose them, as has occurred in the United States (Portney, 1982). In developing countries, which may lack administrative resources, even if environmental quality measures are adopted, such measures may be difficult to police. And many environmental problems have an important international dimension, because many environmental resources extend beyond a single political jurisdiction so that regulations affecting their quality require a negotiated consensus. With weak international cooperation in many fields, including use of resources, it may be unrealistic to expect environmental quality policies established in one country to adequately reflect the potential costs of degradation in another country.

The vast abundance of environmental resources has provided little motive for regulation until relatively recently, when it became increasingly evident that human activity could significantly degrade the quality of environmental resources. In response, the richer countries have instituted policies that have reduced levels and rates of pollution and degradation in most (though not all) major areas of air and water quality (Baumol and Oates, 1984). These improvements reflect the fact that a clean environment is, in a sense, a "luxury good" insofar as the willingness to pay the required costs seems to increase with income levels. For developing countries, there are few systematic time series for measuring environmental quality, but it is clear that important instances of deteriorating quality are occurring (see below).

In discussing the role of population growth in producing change in environmental quality, it is convenient to invoke a scheme used by Commoner et al. (1971). This scheme considers the size of population, the level of per capita production, and the level of pollution produced per unit of production. Commoner and coauthors note that it is pollution per unit of output that has been quantitatively the most important in producing the rising U.S. levels of pollution they review. The second factor, rising levels of per capita production, can have immediate effects that increase pollution, but as noted above, it can also have advantageous effects that work through higher levels of personal income. It is difficult to envision equivalent advantageous effects for changes in population size. Eventually, population growth may increase pollution to the point that new forms of social intervention are introduced, but this possibility does not negate the direct negative effects of population growth.

The most serious international issues reflect economic activity in the developed countries, including the buildup of atmospheric fluorocarbons, carbon dioxide from fossil fuel combustion, and the production of acid rain from sulfurous residues. Although some carbon dioxide accumulation is due to the burning of forests in developing countries, the most important environmental problems in developing countries are likely to be relatively localized, such as air and water pollution from human and industrial waste–especially in cities–and siltation of water resources from erosion. The cumulative effect of localized environmental degradation is difficult to predict because natural processes can clean the air and water up to a certain threshold level, beyond which degradation may progress more rapidly.

How important are these effects in developing countries? Would a developing nation be willing to forgo a small but nonnegligible share of its income or employment growth in order to control or reverse environmental degradation? In many developing countries, air, water, and many species have been treated as free goods. The failure to institute restrictions on the use of these resources suggests either that there are severe technological and institutional barriers to resource control, or that pollution abatement has a low priority relative to a low-income country's other needs. As we noted earlier in the case of oil, as common resources become more scarce and hence more valuable, rules for access to them tend to become better developed and more restrictive.

Means do exist to control at the source the pollution of air and water from industrial processes and the pollution of water in urban areas by human waste. If these means are not implemented, which they apparently are not in Chinese cities, for example (Smil, 1984:100), population growth will likely exacerbate problems of pollution. But the fact that they have not been widely implemented suggests either that the problems are less important, relative to the many other problems of developing countries, or that there are severe technological and institutional barriers to resource control.

The problem of siltation of water resources from soil erosion is exceptional because the means to control it, which originate in millions of actions taken over highly dispersed areas, are not obvious and probably not inexpensive. For example, they are not obvious and inexpensive enough to have been widely adopted in the United States. Crosson (1984) estimates that the off-farm costs of soil erosion in the United States exceed the on-farm costs, largely because of siltation. Crosson (1983) also implies that the same may be true in developing countries, although the data are extremely poor. He cites many instances in developing countries in which the siltation of reservoirs has occurred at a rate far more rapid than anticipated, with a drastic shortening of the economic lives of the reservoirs because of unanticipated increases in soil erosion.

Species loss is another example of a problem difficult to control because of the highly dispersed actions that contribute to it. It is an international problem because the potential usefulness of a particular species is not confined to a single country or ecological area. And unlike many of the other resource problems with an international dimension, species loss is more acute in developing than in developed countries. Tropical areas are the home of about two-thirds of the known species of plants and animals (Harrington and Fisher, 1982). Data on the rate of loss are very poor (Simon and Wildavsky, 1984), but there is little question that the rate of loss has accelerated in recent years and little hope or expectation that the rate of loss in developing countries will diminish in the near future. The rate of loss is unlikely to be slowed because of the difficulty of enforcing preservation strategies and the tendency to heavily discount their aesthetic value as well as a future in which the disappearing species may acquire greater economic value–as food, fiber, building material, and drugs. Population growth, particularly by encouraging encroachment on forested areas, is surely contributing to the loss of species (Myers, 1980; Harrington and Fisher, 1982).

Population may be a factor in climatic change at both the regional and global level. Overgrazing by the herds kept by nomadic peoples in the Sahel region of Africa, for example, apparently led to the loss of ground cover, which increased the sunlight reflected from the earth and reduced the level of rainfall, accelerating the process of desertification (World Meteorological Organization, 1983). The accumulation of atmospheric carbon dioxide and the emergence of the "greenhouse" effect, the economic implications of which are uncertain, depend in part on population growth (National Research Council, 1984). Using the analytical scheme suggested by Commoner et al. (1971), and assuming continued growth in output per capita and dependence on technology based on energy from fossil fuel combustion, rapid population growth in the developing countries will contribute to the buildup. This buildup could hasten the global temperature increases and climatic change now predicted for the latter part of the next century (World Meteorological Organization, 1983). Because forests convert carbon dioxide to oxygen through photosynthesis, the clearing of forest areas for settlement under population pressure also contributes to the greenhouse effect.

CONCLUSIONS

Because environmental resources are common property, they tend to be overexploited, leading to pollution and degradation. Controlling or reversing environmental damage seems to have a low priority in developing countries in view of the substantial fiscal and institutional requirements. Although population growth contributes directly and indirectly to environmental problems, it is important to emphasize that the common-property aspect of environmental resources also contributes to these problems. Damage is likely to continue in the developing countries until environmental resources become scarce enough that the countries are willing to bear the cost of environmental protection and until the corrective social and political institutions develop. It is necessary, of course, that such protection be undertaken before the resource is irreparably damaged. While the long-term solution to these problems will require socially negotiated access rules, slower population growth might allow somewhat more time for developing countries to implement the policies and to develop the institutions necessary to protect the environment.

4

Will slower population growth lead to more capital per worker, thereby increasing per worker output and consumption?

Production of economic goods and services requires the use of various factors in a technical process. One type of factor is physical capital,* including social infrastructure (roads, communications, dams), machinery, buildings, and inventories. Another factor is labor, and it is often important to distinguish between the number of workers and the characteristics that may affect their usefulness in production, often referred to as "human capital."

When production processes exhibit constant returns to scale, in the sense that increasing all inputs by a given proportion increases total output in just that proportion, the average productivity of each worker depends on his or her human capital and the average amount of other factors with which he or she works, but not on the number of workers or the overall amount of any other factor. In this situation, when more of any single factor is used, total production increases but the average output per unit of the increased factor declines, while the average productivity of all other factors increases.

When the growth of the population and labor force is rapid, the growth of the stock of physical and human capital must be equally rapid if a decline in their average quantity per worker, known as "capital dilution," is not to occur. If, in the absence of technical change, capital stocks do not increase in proportion to the growth of the labor force, then real wage rates will decline and per capita income growth may slow or reverse. Conversely, if capital accumulation outpaces the growth of the labor force, wages will

---

*In this chapter, "physical capital" is sometimes abbreviated to "capital" when there is no possibility of confusion with human capital.

increase, and per capita income will also probably increase. However, if investment were too high, consumption might fall because of the high rate of saving required to maintain the level of capital per worker. Technological change may offset the effects of capital dilution; this possibility is discussed in the next section. For the present, however, the possibility of such offsetting change is ignored.

It seems useful to put the role of physical capital accumulation in economic growth in perspective. Physical capital accumulation is sometimes viewed as the critical ingredient for growth, and it is the most easily quantifiable and analyzable of all sources of growth. But its contribution may be quite modest. Denison (1974), for example, found that capital accumulation accounted for only 15 percent of the growth in total income in the United States from 1929 to 1969 and only 11 percent of the growth in per capita income. While some of the balance can be explained by growth in other measured inputs, such as education, much of it (about one-half for total income and about four-fifths for per capita income) remains unexplained and is attributed to such categories as growth in knowledge and returns to scale. Conditions in today's developing countries differ from the historical U.S. context, and Denison's analysis is not necessarily generalizable. However, it illustrates that one should not assume that physical capital accumulation is the principal source of economic growth.

Simple algebra shows that if new workers are to have the same amount of physical capital to work with as those already in the labor force, then the net investment rate, s, must equal the rate of growth of the labor force, n, times the capital/output ratio, e–that is, $s = ne$–which is typically about 3. If the net investment rate exceeds this amount, as it generally does, then the excess is available for increasing the amount of capital per worker ("capital deepening"), thereby raising per capita output. The conceptually separable portion of investment going to meet the needs of new workers (ne) is sometimes called demographic investment, and it is one form of "capital widening" (World Bank, 1974). A stationary labor force would require no demographic investment; one growing at 3 percent annually would require (assuming a capital/output ratio of 3) demographic investment equal to about 9 percent of total annual output. Demographic investment generally forms a far higher proportion of total investment in developing countries than in developed countries because of their more rapid population growth rates and frequently lower rates of savings, although there is much intercountry variation (World Bank, 1974).

If the net investment rate does not change, what is the effect of an increase in the rate of population growth? Initially, net savings would be inadequate to provide new workers with as much capital as existing workers had, so the average amount of capital per worker would fall, leading to lower output and lower per capita income. After a time, however, capital per worker would have fallen sufficiently low to be just sustained by the savings rate, given the growth in the labor force, and no further decline in income would occur. Thus, the population growth rate, acting through capital dilution, should have no further effect at all on the growth rate of per capita income, and any income growth will then depend solely on the rate of technological progress (Solow, 1956; Phelps, 1968). To the extent that countries' economies resemble this theoretical concept, there is no reason to expect any correlation between the population growth rate and the rate of growth of per capita income across countries (Phelps, 1968). Indeed, many empirical cross-national studies have confirmed the absence of such a correlation (see Simon, 1977, for a review).

The theory does not lead one to expect a negative effect of population growth rates on the rate of change of per capita income in the long run. However, if rates of net investment and technological progress are unchanged, it does suggest that more rapid population growth rates will lead to less capital per worker, thereby depressing the level of per capita income. The magnitude of this effect can be easily calculated: per capita income in a population growing at 3 percent per year would be only 13 percent lower than in one growing at 1 percent per year. In both cases, per capita income would be growing at the rate of technological progress.* This calculation reflects the effect of capital dilution alone and is by no means intended to indicate even approximately the entire effect of population growth operating through all channels.

So far, the rate of capital formation has been assumed to be constant or to be adjusted in some exogenous way when the population growth rate changes. But there are a number of reasons to expect that different demographic situations will themselves lead to changes in the rate of capital formation; some of these changes would be expected to exacerbate the problem of capital· dilution rather than mitigate it.

---

*The calculations are based on results in Keeley (1976:25-45) and assume technological progress at 2 percent annually, depreciation at 3 percent annually, and a constant-return-to-scale Cobb-Douglas production function with a capital coefficient of 0.3 and a labor coefficient of 0.7, and a savings rate that is independent of the population growth rate. The economy takes 15 years to adjust halfway to the new steady-state capital/labor ratio following a change in the population growth rate. If instead of requiring the savings rate to be constant, one assumes it to be at the optimal level (i.e., to maximize consumption) for each population growth rate, the results would be unaltered in the Cobb-Douglas case considered here, but more generally, the adverse effects of more rapid population growth would be mitigated. Technological change in this calculation was assumed to be labor augmenting; for the case of embodied capital-augmenting technical progress, see Phelps (1968:499).

It is sometimes argued that more rapid population growth and a younger age structure reduce investment in physical capital by diverting scarce funds to human capital expenditures, such as health and education expenditures, which are argued to have a more delayed effect and a lower rate of return (Coale and Hoover, 1958). However, it is not clear that governments actually do devote a greater share of their gross national product (GNP) to such expenditures in countries whose populations have younger age distributions or more rapid growth rates (see, e.g., Schultz, 1985). But if one supposes that savings must be used to equip each new worker with both human and physical capital, then even if their rates of return were equal, the effects of population growth could be considerably stronger than the calculation above suggests (Kuznets, 1967). For example, if capital, when broadly construed to include human as well as physical forms, is responsible for one-half rather than one-third of output, then the negative effects of population growth, operating through capital dilution, would be twice as large as in the above example.

Domestic savings are an important source of funds for physical capital formation. It is often argued that higher fertility and younger age distributions in a population will increase consumption relative to savings, since each adult will have more children to support. A more sophisticated argument views savings and asset accumulation as a strategy for smoothing individual consumption over the life cycle, including old age, taking into account the greater need for total household consumption when children are present (Mason, 1985; Tobin, 1967).

This approach generates two opposite effects. On the positive side, more rapidly growing populations (if the difference is due to fertility) have a smaller proportion of older people who are dissavers relative to younger workers who are saving for retirement; therefore, such populations will generate positive net savings in the aggregate, even though the average individual dies without a penny. This positive effect of fertility on savings rates is called the rate-of-growth effect and occurs equally when per capita income is growing over time (Mason, 1985). At the same time, higher fertility also has a negative effect, because having more children to support shifts the average timing of household consumption to an earlier age of the head of household and thereby postpones the timing of saving for retirement; it may even lead to a period of dissaving in the early to middle years of the household life cycle (Mason, 1985; Arthur and McNicoll, 1978).

Both these effects are stronger when per capita income is increasing more rapidly. On the basis of theory alone, one cannot predict either a negative or a positive effect of fertility on the aggregate saving rate, although there are clearly good reasons to expect some effect. Differences in mortality also directly affect the population growth rate, but they have only weak effects on the age distribution. Nonetheless, the net effect of mortality and fertility changes on savings should be similar since lower mortality increases life-cycle saving for old age.

These arguments concern the motivations for individual or household saving, but much saving is done by governments and corporations, which calls into question the relevance of household-level theories. To the extent that governments and corporations respond to the preferences of their citizens and stockholders, public and corporate savings will reflect the same demographic influences as do direct household savings. Households may also adjust their private savings to compensate for perceived over- or undersavings by governments or corporations; this possibility would lend further plausibility to the hypothesized links between household preferences and aggregate savings. But these assumptions about the behavior of governments, corporations, and households may not hold in all countries, developed or developing.

There have been a number of empirical investigations of the effect of age composition, represented by ratios of dependent to working-age groups, on aggregate national savings rates. The first and best known was due to Leff (1968), who used a cross-national data set and found that both child and old-age dependency ratios depressed savings rates. Subsequent research has questioned his results, with most commentators claiming that the effect was weaker or nonexistent, but some also claiming that the effect should actually be stronger (Mason, 1985). In a more carefully derived model, Mason (1985) found negative effects of dependency on savings and positive effects of population growth rates on savings, with the net effect of higher fertility being positive when the growth rate of per capita income is zero and negative when it is as high as 4 percent, with a nonmonotonic relationship in the middle range. Hammer (1984) sees fertility and savings as being alternative forms of provision for old age in developing countries, with the development of financial institutions inducing a switch from fertility to savings; in this case, high fertility would accompany low savings, but not cause it.

There have also been a number of household-level studies. These tend to show either no effect of child dependency on savings or a negative effect, for both developed and developing countries (Mason, 1985). Some studies have found that children both reduce the proportion of income saved and lead to an increase in household income, with the two effects offsetting each other so that household savings are substantially unaltered (Kelley, 1973). In interpreting these household studies, it must be remembered that a change in fertility also alters the distribution of households by age of head, leading to effects that may tend to offset effects within households. A consensus view has not yet emerged from the aggregate and household-level research, and one might most safely say that research to date, while sometimes revealing negative effects of higher fertility and younger age distributions on saving rates, does not yet provide a compelling case for such a relationship.

In addition to affecting the age distribution, changes in the population growth rate redistribute income between groups with different savings propensities. Population growth tends to raise returns to land and to capital, and recipients of such income are believed to be wealthier and to have higher savings rates than recipients of labor income. This tendency suggests that if slower population growth boosts wages and decreases rents and profits, the result may be a lower aggregate savings rate.

In the preceding discussion, we have emphasized the savings rate as the chief determinant of investment. In theory, the amount of resources devoted to investment is jointly determined by the supply of savings (chiefly from households) and a demand for investment funds (chiefly by businesses).

Current demand for investment funds is linked to the expected future profit rate, which is believed to be positively linked to the rate of growth of GNP. More rapid growth implies a greater future need for capital equipment and a business environment more conducive to experimentation with new techniques. If investors think that population growth promises GNP growth, investment demand will be stimulated. In turn, an increase in investment demand could raise the interest rate, possibly eliciting additional savings and thereby increasing the proportion of output devoted to investment. However, recent empirical work (based on aggregate savings rates in seven Asian countries over the period 1964-1980) suggests that the supply of savings is relatively insensitive to the interest rate (Giovannini, 1983), which in turn suggests that a change in investment demand would affect the interest rate but not the realized quantity of investment. In sum, the link between population growth and realized investment via increased demand for investment funds is hypothetical and tenuous.

However, population growth may directly improve the average quality or effectiveness of the capital stock. Population growth could increase the rate of growth of the capital stock, decreasing its average age. If new technology is embodied in new capital, then capital may on average be somewhat more productive, partially offsetting the effects of capital dilution.* (The issue of productivity gains from population-induced economies of scale is discussed under Question 5.)

It should also be noted that domestic saving is not the sole source

---

*The average age of capital stock, in a steady state, equals the inverse of the rate of population growth plus that of technology plus depreciation. If technological progress is 2 percent per year and depreciation is 3 percent, then with a population growth rate of 3 percent, the average age of capital would be 12.5 years; with 2 percent, it would be 14.3 years; and with 1 percent, it would be 16.7 years (Phelps, 1962).

of domestic capital formation; international capital flows may also be an important source. Thus, at early stages of a country's development, when its capital endowment relative to labor is relatively small, it can borrow from abroad (or foreigners may invest in its economy) until the domestic rate of return to capital is equal to the foreign rate of return. Rapid population growth may encourage these inflows by boosting the domestic rate of return to capital, thus making investment more attractive. If a country's economy is large relative to that of the rest of the world, it cannot expect to lend or borrow any amount at an unchanging rate of interest; see Deardorff (1985) for a relevant analysis of this case. Whether the country can expect to raise its steady-state per capita consumption above its self-sufficient level by recourse to foreign lending or borrowing will depend, among other things, on its rate of growth of population relative to that of the rest of the world.

CONCLUSIONS

Slower population growth can be expected to increase the ratio of capital to labor, which in turn will increase the level of per capita income. The first link–between population and the capital/labor ratio–has two components. First, holding constant the growth rate of investment in physical capital, theoretical arguments indicate that slower population growth will directly increase the capital/labor ratio. Second, slower population growth could change the rate of saving and investment and thereby change the growth rate of physical capital. While the direction of this effect is indeterminate, there is no evidence to suggest that slower population growth would significantly decrease the savings rate, and some evidence actually suggests a positive effect. Thus we would expect slower population growth to have a net positive effect on the capital/labor ratio. An increase in this ratio, in turn, will increase the level of per capita output, though theory and limited empirical evidence suggest that this effect may be relatively modest. Thus, while capital deepening does appear, at least in theory, to be a genuine positive consequence of reduced population growth, such growth by no means appears to be a decisive influence.

5 Do lower population densities lead to lower per capita incomes via a reduced stimulus to technological innovation and reduced exploitation of economies of scale in production and infrastructure?

The proposition that rapid population growth and greater population density lead to higher per capita incomes has been advanced for both ancient and modern economies and both developing and developed countries. It can also be argued that the possibilities of realizing any economies of scale through international trade and of adapting technology developed by developed countries would make this proposition false for contemporary developing countries. This discussion distinguishes between manufacturing and agriculture and between changes that make it possible to use factors in different proportions and changes that yield more output for factors used in given proportions. It should be noted that there is an important difference between the proposition that greater density is beneficial and the proposition that rapid population growth is beneficial. The beneficial influences of greater density, if they exist, may accrue slowly over time; in the short and medium run, they may be overwhelmed by the costs imposed by rapid population growth. And it may sometimes be possible to capture the benefits of density by concentrating the existing population in a smaller area.

In Denison's (1974) calculations for the United States, changes in all measured economic inputs account for only about 50 percent of total economic growth and 20 percent of growth in per capita income. The remainder Denison classifies as due to advances in knowledge, economies of scale, changes in the efficiency of the allocation of labor, and some additional minor categories. Thus, in order to understand the consequences of population growth, one must understand the influence of those factors on the growth of per capita income.

MANUFACTURING

We begin with the question of whether larger populations may lead to economies of scale in manufacturing. Empirical research has shown that economies of scale in the provision of infrastructural services do exist at the city level and that they are weakly associated with the overall size of the city. They are much more strongly associated with the local size of the particular industries in which the city specializes; these economies of scale are called "localization economies" (Henderson, 1985). Localization economies, which are exhausted above moderate city size, arise from several sources. The easy and rapid exchange of information within an industry facilitates the adoption of new technology, and possibilities of specialization of tasks within the industry emerge. There is also the possibility of drawing on a larger experienced work force. The nature of these economies suggests that national size and population density should be of little relevance, except insofar as they provide a large enough market to allow the industry to reach a sufficient size within at least one city (Henderson, 1985). It is also thought that these localization economies occur primarily for goods that are produced using technology (imported from developed countries) with relatively high capital/labor ratios and that such goods are primarily demanded by the wealthiest segment of the populations in the developing countries. Modern consumer durables are examples of such goods. Thus, the existence of manufacturing economies of scale in developing countries may occur principally when the income distribution is quite unequal. Labor-intensive manufacturing for a low-income mass market might well not experience such economies of scale (James, 1985).

Economies of scale at the national level may also occur. Denison (1974) concluded that for the United States over the period 1929-1969, economies of scale contributed a little more than 10 percent to the increase in income per worker and that their contribution was substantially greater than the contribution of increased capital per worker and nearly as large as the contribution of education. However, the empirical and methodological basis for the calculated scale returns was very weak.

Aside from economies of scale for a given technology, might greater population size or density lead to more rapid technological progress in manufacturing? Without a local capital goods industry, there may be less demand for locally produced technological progress. Larger economies are far more likely to support a local capital goods industry and are therefore more likely to generate indigenous technological progress (James, 1985). Likewise, it has been argued that the rate of technological progress will be positively affected by the number of researchers, which will increase with the size of the total population (Phelps, 1980; Simon and Steinman, 1981).

But these arguments are generally advanced at the global level, and one must ask why a developing country would generate its own technological progress rather than importing technology from developed countries. One answer might be that the technology from developed countries uses much more capital per worker than is appropriate in labor-abundant developing countries. However, it is possible that the imported technology is in fact more efficient in the sense that the productivity of both capital and labor is higher, in which case the argument is undermined. Countries with larger populations and therefore larger markets should, in principle, be better situated to develop technology appropriate to local factor proportions. The argument has been made in great detail that technological change in England—in contrast to the United States—was historically guided in the direction of saving capital rather than labor, reflecting the relative scarcities of factors in these countries (Habakkuk, 1962; David, 1975). In many contemporary developing countries, however, a variety of government policies distort local factor prices so severely that there is no incentive to develop techniques that exploit the relative abundance of labor. Such policies include overvalued exchange rates and credit policies that favor industry and artificially reduce the price of capital goods, particularly those imported from developed countries.

It should be noted, however, that the markets for which final production is targeted may influence the choice of production technique. For example, goods for high-income consumers, for use in the modern economic sector of developing countries, or for export to the developing countries may require relatively capital-intensive production techniques to ensure high levels of standardization or quality (James, 1985). For these reasons, most local technology appears to mirror the factor proportions of developed countries, with a few East Asian countries being the impressive exception (James, 1985).

Similarly, higher national population densities do not appear to offer manufacturing any advantages arising from reduced costs of infrastructural investment since what matters is not national density but rather urban concentration, which today does not depend on overall density, although it might have in the past (Boserup, 1981).

Based on existing research, there is little reason to expect technological progress in manufacturing to be favorably affected by greater population size or density in any individual country, particularly given government policies that are now common. James (1985), in a cross-national sample of developing countries, found no statistically significant association between the rate of industrial labor productivity growth (which reflects changes in capital, the scale of production, and technology) and the population growth rate from 1960 to 1970. Research in this area is in its infancy, and it would be premature to rule out altogether the possibility of positive effects.

AGRICULTURE

Because agriculture is dispersed and carried out in small units under varying agroclimatic conditions, there are no national economies of scale operating through the size of production units. However, it has been plausibly argued that greater population density on agricultural land should favorably influence infrastructural investment in transportation, communications, irrigation, markets, agricultural extension stations, repair shops, and so on, since with denser populations each location can serve more people and therefore have lower per capita costs (Boserup, 1981; Simon, 1977). Limited empirical work supports these arguments (Boserup, 1981; Simon, 1975; Glover and Simon, 1975; but see Evenson, 1984a, who sometimes finds negative effects). Without such infrastructure, the transfer of modern agricultural technology is difficult. For example, irrigation becomes profitable only after a certain density has been reached (note, for example, the failure of many irrigation schemes in sub-Saharan Africa), but in some countries, it is a prerequisite for adoption of many modern, high-yielding plant varieties. Consequently, lower density agricultural populations that have not in the past invested in irrigation may be less well situated to benefit from new agricultural technology (Hayami and Ruttan, 1985; Pingali and Binswanger, 1985).

It also appears to be even more true in agriculture than in manufacturing that each region needs its own technology, suited not only to the relative supplies of land, labor, and capital, but also to the local agroclimatic conditions. Therefore, local research and development are even more important for agriculture than for industry. More densely settled populations would appear to generate a greater demand for such local research and be better able to fund it (Pingali and Binswanger, 1985). Very little empirical research has been done, but Evenson's (1984b) analysis of data from northern India does not support this argument.

It is useful to distinguish three different aspects of technological change: first, change in the basic agrarian system in use, with each system employing factors in different proportions; second, the direction of technological change, in the sense that new knowledge tends to economize on either land or labor within any given agrarian system; and third, the pace of technological change. Examples of agrarian systems, running from least to most intensive use of labor, include forest fallow, bush fallow, grass fallow, annual cropping, and multicropping, each with its distinctive tools and other features. Agrarian systems using the plow are often viewed as more advanced than slash and burn, but they are not necessarily so: each system is most efficient at a particular population density, and farmers have been observed to switch from plow cultivation to slash and burn when density has declined. As the population in an area becomes denser, more labor-intensive systems are adopted if the population changes occur slowly enough so that the appropriate complementary investments in infrastructure can be made and institutional changes can occur (Rosenzweig et al., 1984). Even if technology does not change, returns to labor appear to decline at most quite gently with increasing density, far more gently than they do when labor inputs are increased within any single system (Boserup, 1965, 1981; Pingali and Binswanger, 1985; Hayami and Ruttan, 1985). Declining returns to labor are often offset by increased hours of work.

Within any agrarian system, it may be possible to substitute animal or mechanical power for labor, and irrigation, fertilizer, or new seed varieties for land. This substitution is often effected by technological change. As noted in our discussion of renewable resources, research reveals a close association between population density and the labor intensity of technology, an association that is consistent with the view that the substitution has been historically quite responsive to differences in relative availabilities of land and labor as reflected in their prices (Hayami and Ruttan, 1985; Pingali and Binswanger, 1985). Thus, although the evidence is not conclusive, population growth and density apparently play an important role in directing technological change in agriculture, in contrast to manufacturing, for which technologies and their labor-saving bias typically seem less appropriate to labor abundance (James, 1985). Unfortunately, it is difficult to determine empirically the direction of causation leading to observed associations. And, as in manufacturing, government policies governing prices of inputs and outputs also exert an influence, but in agriculture these are less dominant.

This review of the evidence suggests that population density strongly influences the choice of agrarian system and the direction of technological change. But there is nothing in these arguments to suggest that denser or more rapidly growing populations are better off; rather, they show that the choice of system and direction of technological change typically adjust to the negative effects of higher density and more rapid growth.

These results raise the question of whether countries with denser populations generate a pace of technological advance that gives them a net advantage over those with less dense populations. There are a number of reasons why technological progress in agriculture might be more rapid in denser populations. Some of these derive from the infrastructural advantages of denser populations, which facilitate the flow of information about new technologies and, by increasing the possibilities for marketing output, also increase the gains to, and incentives for, raising productivity. Denser populations may also be better able to bear the fixed costs of agricultural research relevant to an area's particular conditions. If such positive influences on technology do occur over some range of densities, there might well be a point beyond which further increases were disadvantageous.

Analyzing a cross-section of 45 developing countries, James (1985) found that the rate of growth of labor productivity in agriculture between 1960 and 1970 was significantly positively related to the national population density in 1965, while productivity gains in manufacturing were not. While this finding is based on a very rough analysis and should be regarded as very preliminary, it is consistent with the view that density has nonnegligible positive effects on technological advances in agriculture. However, Evenson's (1984b) study of northern India found the negative effects of density on production growth to be about twice as great as the positive ones. A number of other studies have examined the relationship between population density in developing countries and the rate of growth of output per capita or per worker, but very little can be concluded from them. They all report a positive association for at least some range of densities (Lefebvre, 1977; Simon and Gobin, 1980), but in some studies the association becomes negative after densities of about 100 persons per square kilometer are reached.

CONCLUSIONS

In manufacturing, economies of scale exist principally at the urban level and are exhausted at a moderate level of city size. Hence, there is no significant relation between national population density and economies of scale. Moreover, given a widespread dependence on imported technology and the existence of international markets for many manufactured goods, national population density offers little stimulus for technological progress in manufacturing. We therefore conclude that slower population growth would not have any negative effect on productivity in manufacturing.

In contrast, we find that the choice of agricultural technique is responsive to population density. Economies of scale in agriculture are also likely to occur, especially by spreading fixed costs in infrastructure and research over a larger number of people. Although there is no conclusive evidence on this point, there are probably more direct methods for stimulating research and development. It seems unlikely that the stimulative effects of increased population density on agricultural productivity could more than offset the effects of diminishing returns to labor (discussed under Question 2). Thus, for most developing countries, slower population growth is unlikely to result in a net reduction in agricultural productivity and might well raise it.

6 *Will slower population growth increase per capita levels of schooling and health?*

HUMAN CAPITAL AND ECONOMIC DEVELOPMENT

Governments in virtually all developing countries are attempting to increase levels of schooling and to improve levels of health. These goals are also very important to households and other major social units. In addition to their intrinsic value as elements of human welfare, improved health and education contribute to improved economic performance. A better educated work force is more skilled, more adaptable, and more entrepreneurial. The value of education is not limited to any particular sector of the economy: better educated farmers appear more responsive to new technical possibilities, and better educated women seem more effective at allocating resources within the home, including those that enhance child survival (Schultz, 1979; Mensch et al., 1985).

The importance of an educated work force for economic performance has been demonstrated both in studies that attempt to assign economic growth to various components and in studies that attempt to calculate directly the rate of return to completion of additional years of schooling. Denison (1962) attributed 42 percent of the increase in per capita GNP in the United States between 1929 and 1957 to higher average levels of education. A substantial fraction of European economic growth can also be assigned to this source. Educational upgrading contributed substantially to Japan's move from a developing to a developed economy. Denison and Chung (1976) estimate that in the decade 1961-1971 educational advance raised the growth rate of per capita GNP by 0.35 percent per year in Japan. In most of the studies attributing economic growth to various factors, an important residual

53

remains that represents unexplained gains in output for a given level of the factors. It is likely that improved education accounts for a significant part of these improvements.

When rates of return to investment in schooling are computed in developing countries, they invariably are very high. Psacharopoulos (1981) reviews many such computations and finds that the mean social rate of return in 22 developing countries is 27 percent for primary schooling, 16 percent for secondary schooling, and 13 percent for higher education. There are reasons to believe that these figures are biased upward by, among other things, failure to control differences in the ability and class background of persons receiving different levels of schooling. But even when these and other biases are taken into account, the returns to schooling are typically very high (Psacharopoulos, 1981).

The role of health improvements in economic growth has not received as much detailed attention as education. (For a useful review, see Barlow, 1979.) The issue is more complex than that of education because health improvements may also increase rates of population growth, introducing many additional considerations. In a simulation exercise based on the Coale-Hoover model, Barlow (1967) found that the antimalarial campaign in Sri Lanka raised the growth rate of per capita income in the short term, largely because of enhanced labor productivity, but lowered it in the long run, largely because of reduced levels of physical capital per worker (see the discussion under Question 4). Ram and Schultz (1979) suggest that the antimalarial campaign in India during the 1950s was the major reason that income growth rates were higher in that decade than during the widely publicized 1960s, when new crop varieties were introduced. For Sierra Leone, Strauss (1985) finds evidence that family nutritional intake is strongly related to family farm ouput. Deolalikar (1984) provides direct evidence on the economic payoff to improved nutritional status in south India, finding that each percentage point increase in weight-for-height of agricultural workers raised their daily wages by about 1 percent. Whatever the directly measured economic effect, it is certain that health gains would become a larger positive contributor to economic growth if measures of economic growth included an imputation for the value of gains in life expectancy (Usher, 1973).

Because of the contribution of advances in health and education to social and economic development, it is important to identify the effect of population growth on these variables. It should be recognized at the outset that the postwar era of rapid population growth has also been one of rapid gains in educational attainment and life expectancy in developing countries. In the case of life expectancy, improvements have directly contributed to more rapid population growth, a necessary relationship that makes it difficult to use time-series data to infer the importance of the reverse causal paths. What can be said is that the economic response to rapid population growth has not been so negative as to reverse the gains in life expectancy that initiated such growth. The Malthusian specter of population growth precipitating a rise in mortality that restores some kind of economic-demographic equilibrium gains little support from events occurring between 1950 and 1980. Indeed, the incidence of famine-related mortality seems to have declined throughout the twentieth century (World Bank, 1984; Simon, 1981), although famine conditions in China between 1959 and 1961 that have only recently come to light may alter this conclusion (Coale, 1984; Ashton et al., 1984).

While time-series data are instructive in setting some broad parameters within which these processes work, cross-sectional analyses permit a more precise view of the consequences of population growth by taking advantage of richer data that exhibit more independent variation among variables of interest. Such analyses have been carried out both at the family or household level and at the national level. These levels of analysis are not mutually exclusive—nations consist of families and households, and national (or regional) policies affect the decisions made at the household level—but the distinction is widely observed in the research literature.

FAMILY SIZE AND CHILDREN'S HEALTH AND EDUCATION

Family-level relationships between family size and mean education and health of children have been widely reviewed (e.g., Wray, 1971; Terhune, 1974; Birdsall, 1977; Ernst and Angst, 1983; Rodgers, 1984; King, 1985). Beyond a certain family size, additional children are usually associated with lower average educational attainment and reduced levels of child health, as measured by nutritional status, morbidity, and mortality. In addition to the reduced education levels, studies in Hong Kong and India show that school grades among those enrolled tend to be lower for children coming from very large families (Ernst and Angst, 1983:51). However, negative effects of family size on child-quality variables are not always found. For example, Mueller (1984) presents evidence from Botswana and Sierra Leone that children from larger families achieve higher average levels of schooling, controlling other pertinent variables. In general, there are suggestions that the typical negative relationship between family size and health and education of children is larger in poorer families (Birdsall, 1980).

A good deal of recent evidence on the relationship between reproductive patterns and child mortality has become available through the World Fertility Survey. As reviewed by Trussell and Pebley (1984), the evidence suggests that elimination of fourth- and higher-order births in developing countries could reduce infant and child mortality by about 8 percent. Universal adoption of an "ideal" spacing pattern in which all births subsequent to the first are separated by at least 2 years could reduce infant mortality by about 10 percent and child mortality by about 21 percent. (Spacing patterns bear no necessary relationship to population growth, of course, and it is these patterns to which child mortality appears most sensitive.) While the Trussell-Pebley study controlled for certain important socioeconomic variables, it could not control for unmeasured "tastes" for child quality, which would be expected to be stronger among families with few children and long birth intervals. For this reason, the results may represent an upper bound on the child mortality gains to be expected from reduced fertility and longer spacing.

The commonly observed negative relationship between the number of children and the "output" variables of levels of health and education probably reflects a negative relationship between the number of children and various "input" variables. Examples of studies finding negative associations between family size and per capita health and food expenditure can be found in Wray (1971) and Rodgers (1984). It is possible that economies of scale in larger households offset some or all of the disadvantages of lower per capita expenditures, particularly in the area of food provision, although there are few studies confirming such an offset. Reviewing evidence for Kenya, Colombia, and 11 Latin American cities, Tan and Haines (1983) conclude that while total household expenditures on education tend to increase with the number of children, they usually do not increase fast enough to avert a decline in schooling expenditures per child (see Birdsall, 1980, for a detailed discussion of this issue for Colombia). Complicating this relation is the fact that financial support for children's schooling is often derived from older siblings. A majority of fathers in many Asian countries expect such financial help from older sons (Bulatao, 1979), and Caldwell et al. (1982) refer to a common situation in tropical Africa wherein "sibling chains of assistance" are established so that each educated child makes it more likely that the next will be educated. In some places, parents may only have to pay for the advanced schooling of the first child, while later ones are financed by older siblings.

It is important to recognize that no policy implications necessarily follow from a demonstration of a negative cross-sectional relationship between family size and child "quality." Households very often make childbearing decisions with an awareness that having an additional child will entail a sacrifice of some other household objective: leisure, consumption of goods and services, schooling for children already born, health of parents, investment in other household enterprises, and so on. The financial effects of additional children are widely cited concerns in childbearing decisions by families in developing countries (Bulatao, 1979) as well as in developed countries. Obviously, many couples still consider their welfare to be increased by an additional birth despite the costs entailed. Most governments rarely intercede in such decisions, since households themselves bear the brunt of the consequences. And, as illustrated by resolutions passed in United Nations' world population conferences (United Nations, 1984), governments universally proclaim the principle of family sovereignty in reproductive decisions. However, some nations have, in fact, intervened in childbearing processes in ways that violate principles of family sovereignty.

It is also important to note that if a nation achieves lower fertility rates, the impact on the education and health of children will be determined in part by the class distribution of the fertility reduction. If, as widely observed in Latin America, the small upper income groups have the largest proportionate reductions, then the mean levels of child health and education would be expected to decline, other things being equal, even if there are rising expenditures per child by those groups in which fertility declines.

To the extent that a national policy achieves lower fertility levels through family planning programs that reduce the incidence of unwanted children, the question of impact becomes much more highly focused. The class distribution of unwanted births is generally highly skewed toward the lower income groups (Brackett, 1978; Westoff, 1978; Birdsall, 1980). For these groups, it can be anticipated that family planning programs will enhance the mean level of child health and education through compositional effects. One of the few investigations of the effects of an unwanted birth on child quality within families in developing countries is that of Rosenzweig and Wolpin (1980). They find that in India the birth of twins in a household significantly reduces school enrollment levels of children in the household. It also reduces household expenditure on consumer durables. Obviously, not all the twins are unwanted births, but by the nature of the event a higher-than-average proportion are unwanted. Effects on educational enrollments were not confined to the twins themselves but extended to other children in the household. Related studies in India and Thailand using proxies for "wantedness" suggest that child mortality is higher in families in which more unwanted births were occurring (Rodgers, 1984).

POPULATION GROWTH AND
PUBLIC HEALTH AND EDUCATION

In addition to their effects at the family level, levels of fertility can also affect the allocation of government resources to education and health. Educational attainment is produced by some combination of public and private expenditures. At the secondary school level, private contributions often assume greater importance because a child's forgone earnings increase, and governments are less committed to supplying that level of education to large fractions of the population. Effects of population growth on government expenditures can therefore differ from effects on enrollment. Not only do private expenditures play an important and highly variable role, but governments can alter the amount of resources spent on each enrolled child.

Most work on the subject of fertility effects on educational systems is focused on the proposition that more children means that more places must be provided in school systems to maintain the population enrollment ratios. The "costs" of additional children can be readily calculated under reasonable assumptions about per pupil costs (Jones, 1971, 1975; Cochrane, 1983). Jones (1975) shows, for example, that 30-50 percent of the additional governmental education expenditures "required" over the next decade in a typical developing country is attributable to the projected growth of the school-aged population.

These arguments are often among the most convincing to government planning officials about the advantages of reduced fertility. But the fact that enrollment ratios or per pupil expenditures may decline as populations grow does not mean that they necessarily will. Governments can respond to larger school-aged populations in many ways: by raising taxes, by shifting expenditure from other areas, by restructuring educational systems, and so on. Like families, governments are actors in the drama of economic-demographic relations, and their behavior cannot be readily predicted a priori.

The most comprehensive examination of the effects of population growth on educational systems in developing countries is that of Schultz (1985). In a cross-section of countries, Schultz finds that the relative size of school-aged cohorts is negatively associated with government expenditures per school-aged child in both primary and secondary schools. A 10 percent increase in the ratio of the school-aged population to the total population is associated with 11 and 17 percent reductions in expenditures per school-aged child at the primary and secondary levels, respectively. In other words, an increase in the school-aged population induces no increase in total school expenditure and may reduce it. Consistent with this result, there is no association between the relative size of the school-aged population and the share of government expenditures that are directed toward schools.

However, Schultz finds no negative effect of the size of the school-aged population on enrollment rates. In fact, the relationship is positive at the primary level. These results clearly imply that more rapid growth produces lower expenditures per enrolled child, and Schultz shows that this effect takes the form of more enrolled children per teacher and lower teacher salaries. Schultz's results on expenditures are roughly consistent with an earlier cross-sectional study by Simon and Pilarski (1979) that finds a slight negative effect of fertility on expenditure per child. In contrast to Schultz, however, Simon and Pilarski find no effect on primary enrollments and a sizable negative effect of fertility on secondary enrollments.

Although there is much uncertainty in these relationships, it appears that the major effects of population growth on education are on expenditures per pupil–especially teachers per pupil and teacher salaries–and not on enrollment rates. Thus, it is useful to ascertain the importance of expenditures per pupil and teachers per pupil on the quality of education. Intuition strongly suggests that both are positively associated with quality, but the evidence has not always confirmed this intuition. Simmons and Alexander (1978) reviewed multivariate microlevel studies of student performance on standardized tests in developing countries. Two of these studies found a negative or insignificant effect on student performance of per pupil expenditure for school facilities or teachers, and none showed a significant positive effect. Four studies showed a negative or insignificant effect of teacher/pupil ratios, but three showed a positive and significant effect (Simmons and Alexander, 1978:350). These results are similar to those typically found in the United States (Hanushek, 1981; Murnane, 1981).

Additional evidence on this point comes from a study of science test scores among 13- to 14-year-olds in 29 mostly developing countries. Heyneman and Loxley (1983) find that 15-25 percent of the variance in test performance within developing countries can be accounted for by variables representing school and teacher quality. This fraction is larger than is typical for developed countries. The list of quality-related variables is very large and varies from country to country, and it is not possible to generalize to issues of expenditure per child or number of teachers per child. The fact that richer countries tend to have higher test scores in this study also points to the possible importance of school expenditures per child, although influences in the home are also likely to be related to this outcome.

Behrman and Birdsall (1983) examine the effect of school quality (as measured by the mean years of schooling among teachers in one's area during childhood) on adult earnings in Brazil. They find a higher rate of return to investments in school quality than to investments in school quantity. However, they were not able to control for features of the early home environment, which may be related to both quality and quantity of education, and so the net bias is indeterminate.

All these studies show that the quality of schooling can be improved in developing countries (e.g., through providing more textbooks per pupil) and that the savings induced by slower growth of the school-aged population can be used to improve quality. The fact that the aggregate measures of expenditures per pupil and teachers per pupil show only a weak association with test scores in developing countries suggests that one should not be too optimistic that lower population growth will result in improved school quality. But three of seven studies did show a significant positive effect of teacher/student ratios on student test performance, and Schultz's (1985) results suggest that improved teacher/student ratios are the principal route through which lower growth affects education. Therefore, it is reasonable to expect that an exogenous reduction in the growth rate of the school-aged population will in general result in some improvement in quality of education.

Another element in the discussion of the aggregate relation between population growth and the average educational attainment of workers is introduced by Leibenstein (1971:188), who argues: "To the extent that entrants into the work force are of higher quality (i.e., higher education and acquired skills, etc.) than those that leave through retirement and death, the average quality of the labor force improves more rapidly if the rate of population growth is higher (other things equal) than lower." It should be noted that this effect operates only during a transitional period from one demographic equilibrium to another. A once-and-for-all reduction in fertility will lead to a reduced rate of labor force upgrading until a new equilibrium is established. But if a population has constant annual upgrading of amount K in its average endowment of human capital from one cohort to the next (e.g., those aged 15 in 1985 are better endowed by the factor K than those aged 15 in 1984), then regardless of its overall population growth rate, its per capita stock of human capital will be growing at rate K. In equilibrium, there is no relationship between the growth rate of the population and the growth rate of per capita human capital. Even during the transitional period to a lower fertility equilibrium, the welfare implications of Leibenstein's argument are unclear, since all cohorts of individuals are assumed to receive the same schooling in fast-growing populations as in slow-growing populations. It is only the aggregate measures that show a (temporary) deterioration.

There are almost no studies of the effect of demographic variables on government health expenditures. A cursory glance at per capita national health budgets shows extremely wide variations—for example, $16.96 in Mexico and $111.88 in Venezuela (Golladay and Liese, 1980:13)—which probably have more to do with variation in the nature of items that are included in the budgets than with real variations in expenditure. Such figures are not a promising vehicle for empirical investigation without further refinement. However, Montgomery (1985) reports an insignificant, positive effect of population growth rates on government health expenditures as a share of all government expenditures in a cross-section of 49 developing countries.

Whatever the effect of population growth on government health expenditures, those expenditures are not closely related to mortality or health. Nearly all careful studies conclude that government health expenditures per se have very little to do with national health conditions (Corsa and Oakley, 1971; Mosley, 1983). Those health expenditures are usually dominated by urban-based curative services that are often modeled after health systems in developed countries. Not only do these services often fail to reach most of the population, but they also do not appear to improve population-based measures of mortality in the urban populations that they do reach (Mensch et al., 1985). This is not to say that government programs cannot improve health and have not done so, but only that present patterns of expenditure are not such that population growth poses a major threat to success, except, perhaps, in those countries such as Sri Lanka and Cuba, where government health programs appear better constituted and more successful. One way that population growth may actually assist governments in achieving health objectives is by increasing rural density. It is often alleged that, especially in Africa, the dispersed, low-density rural population is difficult to reach with government health services (World Health Organization, 1975:17). These effects have not been adequately quantified.

CONCLUSIONS

We have depicted a multilayered relation between population growth and children's levels of education and health. Several tentative conclusions seem justified. First, larger families generally have lower levels of schooling and health per child, which probably primarily reflects lower expenditures on health, education, and nutrition per child in larger families. However, these relationships are not universal, and they do not necessarily reflect a causal impact of fertility on health and education. Rather, they may to some extent reflect deliberate parental trade-offs between family size and per child expenditure.

Second, family planning programs that decrease the incidence of unwanted births are likely to raise average levels of education and health among children, both because they increase investment within the family in child health and education and because they reduce the fraction of births occurring in lower income families.

Third, countries with more rapid population growth do not appear to have lower levels of school enrollment, ceteris paribus; they do seem to have lower school expenditures per child and fewer teachers per student. Several (but not all) studies have found that having fewer teachers per student reduces student test performance. Therefore, some improvements in test performance may occur as a result of slower population growth.

Finally, it is unlikely that rapid population growth is a major impediment to the success of government health programs as they are presently structured.

7

Will slower population growth decrease the degree of inequality in the distribution of income?

Given a certain level of per capita income, greater variance in the distribution of income generally entails a larger percentage of a population living below whatever absolute income standard defines the poverty line. Consequently, a reduction of income disparities has become a widespread goal of development policy. These disparities can be measured with respect to identifiable characteristics such as occupation or region or with respect to income itself. In the latter case, standard measures such as the Gini coefficient express the amount of inequality in income distribution. Measures of income inequality are to be sharply distinguished from measures of poverty, which focus on households and persons with incomes below some defined income level. From the perspective of developing countries, the likely effect of changes in population growth on poverty is far more important than the effect on inequality, but in this discussion we confine our attention to income inequality.

Although the distributional measures are standard, there is considerable ambiguity about their interpretation. One important question is whether inequality should be measured on a per capita basis or on a per household basis. Since larger households in developing countries tend to have higher total incomes but lower per capita incomes (Srinivasen and Bardhan, 1974; Kuznets, 1976), results can be quite sensitive to the choice of the unit of measurement. Further ambiguity is present because measures of income

This chapter is based heavily on Lam (1985).

62

inequality can actually increase as a result of poorer households suddenly becoming richer. Also, some economic decisions (e.g., the decisions of low-income families to have another child) can result in both increased welfare and increased income inequality.

When inequality is measured with respect to income itself, very little of a general nature can be said about the effects of population growth (i.e., higher levels of fertility). Lam (1985) discusses why empirical time-series and cross-national analyses have not been and are not likely to be fruitful in this area. Nevertheless, some relatively straightforward conclusions can be drawn from theoretical analyses on the assumption that fertility change in a household does not alter its total income.

In the short term, the effects of fertility change depend heavily on the class distribution of that change. If the fertility change is differentiated by income class, per capita measures of inequality can change even in the short term. If lower income groups have proportionally larger fertility declines, then per capita income inequality will decrease. (This relationship holds generally but not universally; Lam, 1985.) If higher income groups have proportionally larger declines, as is often observed in the early stages of a fertility decline (Potter, 1978), then per capita income inequality will increase. When a fertility change is induced by a government-sponsored family planning program, the effects just described will be exaggerated: subsidized family planning services are themselves a form of income to the household, and whichever income groups take greater advantage of the services will have not only higher per capita incomes in the short term, but also greater increases in imputed income from increased service availability. On the other hand, if the fertility decline is induced by setting quantity limits on the number of children per couple, the unmeasured effect of the policy could offset measured changes in income distribution: for example, if high fertility is a greater economic benefit to poorer classes, the imposition of quantity limits could aggravate their poverty (Rodgers, 1984:171).

Longer term effects of fertility change on income distributions are far more complex. They depend on the income-class distribution of the "extra" births and on the income classes of those children when they become adults. They also depend on the impact of those births on aggregate rates of return to various factors of production. On this matter, economic theory is relatively clear, and evidence supports the theoretical predictions: increases in the supply of labor relative to other factors of production (capital and natural resources) are expected to reduce the rate of return to labor and increase the rate of return to other factors of production, other things being equal. Since high-income groups generally own a disproportionate amount of the other factors of production, their incomes can be expected to rise disproportionately, making the population's income more unequally distributed. These effects are expected so long as a decrease in the ratio of wage rates to the price of another factor results in a less-than-proportional substitution of labor for the other factor (see Lam, 1985). Evidence suggests that this is the case (Lam, 1985). Eventually, the greater returns to capital induced by higher fertility can lead to more investment and lower returns to investment, so that effects in the very long term, after all adjustments are completed, can be moderated.

In our discussion of renewable resources (Question 2), historical evidence from England was cited that suggests that population growth had the predicted effects of driving down wages and raising returns to owners of land. Evenson's (1984b) results for northern India suggest the same effect there. Khan (1984) finds evidence that population growth has reduced agricultural wages in Bangladesh, leading to a sharp increase in landlessness and agricultural poverty; in other Asian countries, the effects were not nearly so apparent, probably because industrialization proceeded at a more rapid pace in those countries than in Bangladesh. Unless population growth slows the rate of investment substantially, the "Bangladesh effect" need not arise.

Similar mechanisms can be expected when workers are disaggregated into skilled and unskilled groups, educated and uneducated groups, or finer categories. Because workers of different types are not perfect substitutes for one another (see Kelley and Williamson, 1984), relative increases in one type of worker would decrease wages for that type relative to workers of another type. Williamson and Lindert (1980) examine evidence on inequality in the United States and find that changes in measured inequality reflect closely the changes in wage differences between skilled and unskilled workers, which in turn are a positive function of the rate of population growth. They conclude that faster population growth has produced greater income inequality in the United States, with a major role played by faster population growth depressing relative wages. Behrman and Birdsall (1985) find similar effects in Brazil: wages of unskilled workers are lower, all other things being the same, if they are members of an unusually large cohort. Relative to the wages of unskilled workers, earnings of well-educated workers are increased by membership in a large cohort.

In addition to these effects, which essentially operate through private markets, the effects of population growth on income inequality may also be mediated by government programs. Many government programs are redistributive in their net tax and expenditure effects. If population growth alters the scope or characteristics of these programs, it can change income distribution. Little is known about these relationships. In a cross-national study, Kelley (1976) finds that total government expenditure as a share of GNP is insignificantly affected by the relative size of the youth cohort but strongly and positively associated with the relative size of the elderly cohort. Total expenditure is also negatively but weakly related to the total size and density of the population, perhaps because only central government expenditures are included, and they can be expected to decline as a fraction of all government expenditures when a country's population grows larger. In any event, the net implication of Kelley's results seems to be that government expenditures as a fraction of GNP will rise as population growth declines. In the preceding chapter, we reviewed evidence suggesting that government school expenditure per school-aged child rises when fertility falls, which supports the notion that there may be redistributional gains from declining fertility that are mediated by government programs.

Population growth can affect inequality as measured in other dimensions. For example, intergenerational inequality can be altered by varying levels of fertility. In one sense, all the questions we consider in this volume bear on the issue of intergenerational equality, since we are asking how the future will differ from the present when fertility is lower instead of higher. The fact that the number of members of the next generation is being jointly determined (in part) with its average level of welfare adds great ambiguity to the issue of intergenerational equality. Few people would consider a future generation to be better off if it consisted of only one member with princely wealth; a discussion of the difficulty of making social choices when both numbers and conditions are involved can be found in Dasgupta (1985).

A more tractable issue relates to inequality by sex. In most countries, women bear most of the time, health, and energy burdens of bearing and raising children. When this burden is increased by unwanted children, there is probably a greater welfare loss for women than for men. Programs to improve contraception are thus likely to raise the welfare of women relative to men; in most societies, such a change would produce a reduction in sexual inequality.

CONCLUSIONS

So long as the process of income generation is independent of fertility, the short-term effects of altered fertility on per capita measures of income inequality depend primarily on differences in the amount of fertility change by income class. These differences cannot be predicted a priori. To the extent that publicly supported family planning programs are targeted at the poor and permit them to exercise greater fertility control than they otherwise might, per capita income inequality will be reduced. Longer term effects, which have mainly been investigated in the economic histories of now-developed countries, tend to confirm theoretical predictions that slower population growth will decrease income inequality by increasing the rate of return to labor relative to returns to other factors of production.

8 Will slower population growth facilitate the absorption of workers into the modern economic sector and alleviate problems of urban growth?

THE RELATIONSHIP BETWEEN ECONOMIC DEVELOPMENT AND CITIES

The impact of rapid population growth on the share of the labor force employed in the modern economic sectors of the developing countries and the problems of congestion, slums, and inadequate public services associated with the rapid growth of cities in developing countries are not readily distinguished. Urban labor markets and city growth interact with one another and with other markets and are affected by public policy so that the overall role of population growth cannot be easily determined.

In considering the effect of population growth on labor markets and urban conditions in developing countries, one might define the overall development process in terms of three related processes. Perhaps most fundamental is the structural transformation of economic activity from agriculture or other primary production to industry and modern services, including those provided by the government sector. Because the modern economic sectors are characterized by higher wages, this shift contributes to per capita income growth, the second main feature of development. Finally, both rising income levels and increased public expenditures contribute to access to modern education and improved health care, the third main feature of development.

Cities play an important role in all three aspects of the development process. Both industrialization and the provision of public service infrastructure in developing countries have been largely concentrated in major cities, in part reflecting the economies of scale made possible by urban agglomeration.

The expansion of relatively high-wage modern sector employment and better access to health and educational facilities has attracted rural migrants to cities. While urban-based development provides benefits otherwise unavailable to many people in developing countries, there are also significant costs. Accelerating city growth has strained the capacity of the modern sector to absorb new workers and increased the number of urban poor, contributing to the slums and urban squalor that are among the most visible problems associated with poverty.

POPULATION GROWTH, CITY GROWTH, AND URBANIZATION

Because of their different relationship to the development process, city growth rates and increases in urbanization must be carefully distinguished. City growth rates are the percentage change in the absolute number of people living in a given city or group of cities; increases in urbanization refer to a growing proportion of a national population living in urban areas. It is also useful to differentiate between urbanization patterns exhibiting a high degree of primacy, in which a large proportion of all urban residents live in the largest city, and more diffuse patterns.

An empirical distinction between increasing urbanization and city growth is provided by a comparison of the experiences of developing countries between 1950 and 1975 with that of the now-developed countries between 1875 and 1900. Preston (1979:196) observes that the increase in urbanization for developing countries from 16.7 to 28.0 percent during the recent period is quite similar to the increase from 17.0 to 26.1 percent for the earlier 25-year period. In contrast, cities in developing countries grew at a 4.3 percent annual rate between 1950 and 1975, nearly tripling their urban populations (United Nations, 1980:Table 4) and far exceeding the 2.8 percent average growth rate of cities in the now-developed countries during the late nineteenth century (United Nations, 1980:Table 3). This city growth directly reflects population growth rates of 2.3 percent annually for developing countries over the period (Bureau of the Census, 1983:Table 8), more than double the 1.1 percent rate estimated for the developed countries in the earlier period (United Nations, 1980:Table 4).

Indeed, roughly 60 percent of the growth of cities in developing countries between 1960 and 1970 can be attributed to natural increase (United Nations, 1980:Table 11), and the rate of national population growth appears to be the single most significant determinant of city growth rates. Controlling for other factors, a 1 percent increase in a national population growth rate generates roughly a 1 percent increase in the growth rate of the cities in a country (United Nations, 1980:Table 19), while national political capitals tend to grow more rapidly than do other cities. Higher city growth rates are also associated with more rapid increases in per capita GNP. The importance of national population growth as a determinant of city growth reflects the fact that broad cultural, social, and economic factors tend to determine fertility and mortality within both rural and urban areas in a country. The relatively young age of rural migrants to cities means a greater contribution to natural increase through more births and fewer deaths. This effect tends to offset the declines in fertility rates typically associated with urban residence (Stolnitz, 1984), so that urban rates of natural increase (the difference between birth and death rates) approximate national rates.

In contrast to the relationships between city growth and overall population growth, cross-national studies consistently suggest that urbanization is primarily related to the level of economic development as measured by per capita income or GNP (Chenery and Syrquin, 1975:Table 7). On the basis of recent data, Montgomery (1985) finds urbanization to be much more strongly associated with per capita income than with population growth. The principal demographic source of increasing urbanization is rural-urban migration. Although rapid population growth was once thought to be an important cause of rural-urban migration, with rural poverty due to excess labor supply providing a "push" to the cities (e.g., Lewis, 1954), rural outmigration now seems to be less strongly associated with rural population increase than with changes in agricultural productivity and rates of overall economic growth (United Nations, 1980:Table 13) and to be related to land tenure systems with marked inequality in land holdings and landlessness (Standing, 1984). In fact, Preston (1979) argues that poverty tends to preclude migration, which requires resources, while increasing agricultural productivity generates rural income growth and the means to move. At the same time, expanding industrial output and employment provides an economic "pull" to major cities. This pattern is broadly consistent with the historical experience of the now-developed countries, where the large-scale migration from rural areas to cities occurred in the context of rapid industrial expansion and agricultural productivity growth.

There is strong empirical support for the notion that rural-urban migration in developing countries is motivated primarily by economic opportunity in cities, including both higher wages and access to public services and educational facilities (Greenwood, 1969, 1971, 1978; Schultz, 1971; Yap, 1977; Todaro, 1980; Rempel, 1981; Mazumdar, 1985). Recent simulation studies using models of urbanization by Kelley and Williamson (1984) and Mohan (1984) incorporate linkages between structural economic change, technological growth, and migration. These studies suggest that increasing urbanization in developing countries reflects the growth of industry and modern sector services, while population growth has only a small effect.

In summary, the evidence seems to indicate that the rapid growth of cities in developing countries compared with historical patterns results primarily from high national rates of population increase, while increases in urbanization, which have been roughly comparable with historical experience, are due almost entirely to rural-urban migration in response to economic growth and access to publicly provided services.

URBANIZATION AND ECONOMIC GROWTH

Urban areas play a strategic role in development. To make the best use of scarce public sector resources by exploiting economies of scale, facilities for power generation and water treatment, transportation systems, and other public infrastructure tend to be located in urban areas (United Nations, 1980:39). Access to urban infrastructure confers a cost advantage to industrial firms locating in those areas, as do the economies of scale associated with access to larger and more diversified markets for labor and other input factors, although these economies of scale seem to be attributable more to the clustering of similar industries than to urban size itself (Henderson, 1985).

As industrial output increases, so does the share of relatively high-wage industrial employment. Saving tends to increase as a result of the consequent improvement in average income, providing funds for investment in industrial capital, education (Chenery and Syrquin, 1975:23), and housing stock, the latter representing about 20 percent of all fixed investment and 37 percent of construction in developing countries (Linn, 1983:Table 5-3). As incomes increase, the composition of domestic demand tends to shift from food to nonfood goods, including modern health care and housing services, as well as to manufactured goods, further stimulating modern sector growth (Chenery and Syrquin, 1975:32). With continued changes in the composition of output and consumption, the agricultural share of employment declines, and the share of industry and services increases (Chenery and Syrquin, 1975:48).

Migration in search of higher wages continues in response to expanding modern sector employment, accompanied by increasing urban population densities. In turn, the price of urban land rises (Ingram, 1980), driving up the cost of housing, transported food, and other urban living expenses. This narrows the real rural-urban wage gap, slowing migration and the pace of urbanization (Kelley and Williamson, 1984). As development proceeds, modern sector economic activity diversifies, and the urban sector diffuses into an integrated system of cities, each tending toward specialization in some set of economic activities (Henderson, 1984, 1985). In this highly stylized description, urbanization contributes to overall development by attracting human resources to activities with greater economic returns. The movement of labor from relatively low-wage rural activity to higher-wage industrial and modern service sectors contributes to higher overall average income levels, further stimulating economic growth.

Although contemporary urbanization rates in developing countries are comparable with those in the now-developed countries at the end of the nineteenth century, the proportion of the nonagricultural labor force engaged in manufacturing is significantly lower in today's developing countries than in their historical counterparts–approximately 40 percent in 1981 (World Bank, 1983b:148) compared with 55 percent in 1900 (Squire, 1981:Table 1). This difference raises the question of whether developing countries have been less successful in absorbing labor supply growth into the modern sector. One reason cited for the lower proportion of industrial employment in developing countries relative to the comparable period in the history of the now-developed countries is the labor-saving bias in the former, in spite of abundant labor (Todaro and Stilkind, 1981). Indeed, industrial labor productivity in the developing countries grew at an annual rate of 4.6 percent in the 1960s, compared with a 2.0 percent rate for the relevant countries during the last 20 years of the nineteenth century. This productivity difference reflects the predominance of technology imported or copied from developed countries (James, 1985) and seems to be especially prominent in countries emphasizing domestically manufactured import substitutes, which apparently require more capital-intensive methods than does export-oriented manufacturing (Krueger, 1978).

The relationship between productivity growth and labor absorption in industry is not simply technological. In developing countries, high-quality goods for high-income domestic consumers, for export markets, or as inputs to their growing modern sectors may entail relatively capital-intensive production processes. Expanding industrial output to meet demand in these markets might increase employment enough to offset any decreases in unit labor requirements due to productivity gains (Squire, 1981:29). Moreover, the direct effect of labor-saving technology on industrial employment growth is partly offset by the indirect effect on employment growth in supply sectors when interindustry linkages are taken into account, an effect that tends to be larger as the economy-wide level of technology increases (Stern and Lewis, 1980). Thus, Mohan (1984) suggests that a shift to more labor-intensive production might increase modern sector labor absorption, but the quantitative impact probably would not be large.

Perhaps more relevant to the seemingly slow absorption of labor into industry in the developing countries relative to the history of the last century is the emergence of large government sectors throughout the world in the twentieth century. Publicly provided goods and services are very important in the developing countries, comprising 26.2 percent of gross domestic product

(GDP) expenditures in 1981, even more than the current 21.7 percent for developed countries (World Bank, 1983a:Table 3). Although the service sector typically exhibits lower wage levels than the industrial sector (Squire, 1981:Table 15), so that the shift from agriculture into services rather than into manufacturing slows the growth in average urban income, public sector wages are generally high in developing countries (Squire, 1981:118). On the whole, the share of service employment is consistent with the increasing importance of the service sector in all economies. For example, in the developed countries, industrial workers accounted for only about 40.2 percent of nonagricultural employment in 1981 (World Bank, 1983b:148), roughly the same as the developing countries.

The broad patterns of structural change that characterize the development process are closely related to increasing urbanization. The evidence suggests that, on average, the composition of the urban-based labor force in developing countries is comparable to that of contemporary developed countries, even though the adoption of high-productivity technology may have resulted in a smaller share for industrial employment than historically in the now-developed countries. Moreover, that technology has made possible rapid GDP growth and relatively high industrial wages, generating the tax revenues necessary to expand public services (Chenery and Syrquin, 1975:Tables 4,5,6).

RAPID POPULATION GROWTH AND LABOR MARKETS

A widely noted characteristic of urban labor markets in developing countries is some degree of segmentation. The modern sector generally consists of physical and human capital-intensive industrial and service activities and pays relatively high wages, while the "informal" sector consists of labor-intensive small manufacturing or service businesses and self-employed workers, typically requiring fewer skills and paying relatively low wages. According to Squire (1981:79) a key distinction between the sectors is that the rate of return to labor in informal activities is determined primarily by supply and demand conditions, whereas market imperfections tend to limit modern sector wage flexibility, generating unemployment and supply spillovers to the informal sector. Perhaps because of these rigidities, rapid population growth is associated in cross-national results with a slower absorption of the labor force into industrial and modern sector activities (Oberai, 1978; Squire, 1981:183; Chenery and Syrquin, 1975:48).

Squire (1981:109) cites several possible sources of labor market imperfections in the modern sector, including wage inflexibility in government employment and in large-scale production firms, especially those under foreign control, and a tendency for wage patterns established in those segments of the economy to diffuse throughout the modern sector. He suggests, however, that minimum wage legislation and unions generally tend to exert less impact in developing countries than in developed countries because of their limited scope, although their influence varies across countries. Mazumdar (1984, 1985) notes that large-scale production firms may be motivated to pay a wage premium to encourage worker productivity and ensure stability, given the relative scarcity of skilled workers and the costs of training. Another imperfection is discrimination based on race, ethnicity, and sex, which may also restrict access to high-wage employment (Knight and Sabot, 1982). But while there is evidence of market imperfections, it would be a mistake to conclude that supply factors have no impact on modern sector wage levels. Indeed, there is evidence that, as theory would predict, rapid labor supply increases result in slower wage growth in manufacturing and in other nonmanufacturing modern sector activities (Squire, 1981:Table 16).

Given an urban labor market segmented into relatively high- and low-wage sectors, it may be economically rational for job seekers to accept a period of unemployment while searching for a high-wage job rather than work in the low-wage sector (Todaro, 1969; Harris and Todaro, 1970; Fields, 1975; Harris and Sabot, 1982). Reflecting the relatively rapid expansion of education in developing countries (Squire, 1981:130), open unemployment seems to be highest among young, relatively well-educated labor market entrants whose search for modern sector employment is financed by nonlabor income, typically transfers from family members (Squire, 1981:3). Although data limitations make it difficult to assess the scope of open unemployment, the evidence available suggests that rapid labor force growth in developing countries has not been accompanied by systematic increases in joblessness (Sabolo, 1975; Gregory, 1980).

In contrast to relatively well-off job seekers able to afford unemployment during a search for modern sector employment, most low-skilled urban workers are obliged to accept employment in the informal sector (Linn, 1983:37). Since some employment in this sector represents spillover from modern sector labor markets unable to absorb growth in the urban labor force, it has been characterized as underemployment or disguised unemployment (e.g, International Labour Organisation, 1974). These terms seem to suggest that informal sector activity contributes little to the development process, but there is evidence that many of these activities play useful intermediary roles in modern sector production and distribution (Linn, 1983:40; Montgomery, 1985). Portes and Benton (1984) argue that contractually hired labor raises labor costs and reduces flexibility, so that direct hiring of casual labor or subcontracting to small informal sector businesses may represent an efficient strategy for modern sector firms in construction, light manufacturing, and commercial distribution. While average wages tend to be lower in the informal sector, entrepreneurs may earn incomes comparable to modern sector workers

(Squire, 1981:140), and low wages for less experienced workers may be offset by skill acquisition and eventual accession to self-employment (Montgomery, 1985). In this sense, the interpenetration of informal and modern sector activities may represent a relatively efficient adaptation to institutional factors, contributing to overall employment and economic growth.

At the same time, the relatively free play of supply and demand that characterizes informal sector labor markets means that labor force growth influences wage levels. Because informal sector output is generally not traded internationally, prices of output tend to decline with increases in supply (Squire, 1981:135), so that rapid labor force growth in this sector tends to depress the wages and incomes of people employed in those activities. Indeed, Portes and Benton (1984:589) emphasize that low wages in the informal sector are the prime cause of the income inequality and poverty of urban populations in developing countries.

Even though rapid labor force growth typically results in lower wages than would otherwise prevail in urban labor markets, both in the modern and informal sectors, it is important to note that most urban workers are probably at least as well off as they might be in rural areas. Recent research suggests that migrants to cities are often able to increase their incomes relative to rural levels and, over time, achieve earnings comparable to those of nonmigrant urban residents (Yap, 1977; Squire, 1981:103; Rempel, 1981:93); however, rural-urban living cost differences make comparisons difficult. Of course, the population movement may partly reflect a greater tendency to migrate among those with education or skills most suited to urban job markets or with prior access to job contacts through kinship or village networks (Mazumdar, 1985). Although the return of unsuccessful migrants to rural areas may upwardly bias estimates of the economic returns to migration, Montgomery (1985) concludes that most urban migrants gain economically from their move.

THE EFFECT ON LABOR ABSORPTION OF DISTORTIONS IN OTHER MARKETS

In major urban areas, direct subsidies for food, along with the subsidized provision of infrastructure and health and education services at prices that do not reflect their costs to the public sector, artificially lower living costs. By increasing real rural-urban wage differentials beyond what results from differences in sectoral labor productivity, these subsidies increase migration to cities (Squire, 1981:107). If, as a result, urban labor supply increases more rapidly than modern sector labor demand, unemployment and spillovers to the informal sector may result. Excessively subsidized and inappropriate services may be particularly pronounced in a country's political capital, which is often its largest city (Gilbert, 1976). These distortions would be expected to increase the attractiveness of these cities to migrants, and, in fact, migration seems to be disproportionately important in the growth of this class of cities (United Nations, 1985).

Ceilings on interest rates in developing countries tend to ration credit so that it is available only to a few favored firms, limiting investment that would expand the size of the modern sector. In addition, credit rationing tends to rule out investment by smaller, more labor-intensive enterprises, which would tend to increase informal sector wages (Squire, 1981:166).

Trade policies, including exchange-rate distortions and systems of taxes, subsidies, and quotas favoring some industrial sectors, may have an impact on labor absorption. For example, Chenery and Syrquin (1975:64,116) distinguish two basic trade strategies: import substitution and export-oriented manufacturing. Large developing countries with significant primary resources have typically followed the former strategy, using overvalued exchange rates and taxes on primary exports to subsidize imported capital goods, with quotas or protective tariffs on imported goods that are also manufactured domestically. The effect of such policies is to turn the terms of trade against agriculture, reduce rural output, and increase rural-urban wage differentials, urban migration, and the pace of urbanization (Squire, 1981:153; Todaro and Stilkind, 1981:11). The most significant of these policies is probably exchange-rate distortions (Montgomery, 1985).

At least in partial contrast, some smaller developing countries without important primary resources have followed more export-oriented trade policies that are based on foreign investment in domestic industry and undervalued exchange rates that make exports relatively inexpensive in international markets. An export-oriented trade policy seems to foster not only more rapid industrial growth (Chenery and Syrquin, 1975:42), but also somewhat more rapid growth in the high-wage industrial sector and lower overall unemployment (Squire, 1981:144). One reason for this outcome may be that export-oriented industries tend to exploit labor cost advantages by using technology more labor intensively (James, 1985). In addition, exchange rate undervaluation tends to keep domestic agricultural prices relatively higher, reducing rural-urban wage differentials and slowing migration.

URBAN GROWTH, HOUSING, AND PUBLIC SERVICES

Urbanization has provided access to the benefits of development for an increasing proportion of the population of developing countries. Linn (1983), who provides the best data available, notes that because modern sector economic activity is concentrated in cities, urban residents have access to higher-wage employment and hence enjoy higher per capita incomes (Linn,

1983:Table 1-4) and have a lower incidence of poverty (Linn, 1983:10) than rural residents. Similarly, reflecting both urban economies of scale in the provision of public services and higher income levels, city residents have greater access to electricity (Linn, 1983:Table 1-8), to water supply and sewage removal (Linn, 1983:Table 1-9), to health services as measured directly by doctors per person (Linn, 1983:Table 1-14), to hospital beds (Linn, 1983:Table 1-15), and to education (Linn, 1983:Tables 1-17, 1-18).

However, averages do not tell the whole story. A significant proportion of the urban population lives at low income levels in squatter communities with inadequate access to public services like water, sanitation, education, and health care. Data assembled by Linn (1983:Table 1-7) suggest that the proportion of urban residents living in squatter settlements is rarely less than 25 percent and often more than 50 percent, and he argues that living conditions in these areas are distinctly worse than in nonsquatter areas.

The importance of housing in developing countries is reflected by the large share it represents of the household budget, averaging between 15 and 25 percent of total expenditures (Linn, 1983:Table 5-2). Housing needs include the services derived from the lot and structure, including infrastructure services such as electricity and water. But as land prices increase, both lot size and shelter space tend to decrease, and in conjunction with the large family sizes that are typical of rapidly growing populations, risk of contagious disease increases. Similarly, since squatter settlements often spread to land without public infrastructure, access to safe water and sanitary facilities is limited, also increasing the risk of disease (Linn, 1983:194). Because squatter settlements represent unplanned urban expansion and the provision of public transportation tends to favor authorized, primarily middle-class neighborhoods, access by the poor to health and educational facilities and to employment opportunities is limited. By constraining the ability of the poor to improve their own or their children's stock of human capital, low-quality housing in squatter settlements tends to perpetuate the cycle of urban poverty, effects that may be most severe in the most rapidly growing cities (Linn, 1983:134).

Urban transportation systems, especially road networks, play an important role in economic growth by providing producers and consumers with access to markets, as well as by providing the labor force with access to workplaces. The cost of urban transportation tends to increase with city size because of the increasing costs of land (Linn, 1983:99), so that the public provision of roads tends to lag behind urban population growth. Consequently, congestion increases, increasing trip times and transportation costs (Linn, 1983:90). This increase may disproportionately affect informal sector activities such as small-scale trading and cartage. Moreover, as congestion increases, pollution from motorized transportation also tends to increase (Linn, 1983:98).

Again, not all urban problems in developing countries should be attributed to rapid population growth. Fragmented financial markets and interest-rate ceilings that ration credit in favor of high-income borrowers tend to limit the supply of housing, directly contributing to the growth of squatter settlements (Linn, 1983:133; Renaud, 1982). Rent control laws and inflexible zoning and subdivision regulations also tend to restrict the supply of housing, and, when nonresidential land is invaded by squatters, risk of eviction limits the quality of shelter constructed (Linn, 1983:167). Moreover, publicly funded housing and health care projects are often modeled after relatively high-cost prototypes in developing countries, effectively barring the low-income majority from access (Linn, 1983:138).

CONCLUSIONS

This review emphasizes the distinction between increasing urbanization and population growth to simplify the complex relationships between these demographic processes, labor markets, and the benefits and costs of large cities in developing countries. Urbanization, produced primarily by rural-urban migration, plays an important beneficial role in the development process, providing an increasing share of the population with access to relatively high-wage employment, education, health care, and other modern public services.

But rapid urbanization, resulting from both natural population increases and rural-urban migration, may cause social adjustment and congestion costs that are not fully taken into consideration by the potential migrant, and thus migration may be excessive from a social viewpoint. The most obvious and pervasive reasons for *excessive* urbanization, in contrast to the redeployment of labor and capital to *efficient* opportunities for growth in urban areas, are the many distributive effects of the public sector. Taxes, trade restrictions, and subsidies tend to favor urban residents, and the provision of health, education, and housing services are markedly skewed toward residents in urban areas in most developing countries.

The documentation of the social adjustment costs imposed on economies by rapid rates of urban population growth has proved empirically difficult. Gregory (1980) could find little evidence that urban unemployment had increased in the 1970s as the postwar acceleration in population growth led to more rapid growth of the urban labor force. Nor has evidence yet been presented to show how the composition of the labor force has adapted in recent years to the presumed strains of absorbing many new urban labor force entrants. Documentation is also lacking for presumed diseconomies of scale in service provision and health conditions for very large cities. Even though population growth has undoubtedly exacerbated some urban problems, strained providers of subsidized services, and possibly slowed the growth of the share of workers who are in the modern wage sector, slower population growth will probably not, by itself, solve these problems. A first step toward slowing excessive urban growth would involve reducing the public sector's disproportionate subsidies for urban residents and urban-based economic activities.

9 Can a couple's fertility behavior impose costs on society at large?

A key policy question in considering population growth is whether a couple's childbearing decisions impose costs on, or provide benefits for, other families. If such externalities (effects external to the decision maker) exist, there may be a role for public policies that seek to incorporate the social costs and benefits of fertility into private decisions about family size. As in the case of pollution externalities (see Question 3), an argument can be made that equating social and private costs yields gains that could potentially increase the well-being of all members of society.

In considering this question, there is an important distinction to be made between true externalities and pecuniary externalities. True externalities are external costs and benefits that are not mediated through markets. For example, because access to the air is unrestricted, manufacturers do not factor into their production decisions the costs imposed on others by their air pollution. It is possible to envision systems of property rights that would either give people the right to clean air or manufacturers the right to pollute. Under either system, trading of the rights would theoretically result in an optimal level of pollution, at which the social costs of an additional unit of pollution would equal the social gains of the associated increment of production. Thus, introduction of property rights, or of government regulations that achieve the same end, results in a net gain to society. Of course, the manner in which these gains are distributed depends on the way property rights are defined and allocated, but in principle the gains could be distributed so as to make everyone in society better off. For this reason, welfare economics unambiguously recommends policy intervention to correct market failures resulting from true externalities.

In contrast, pecuniary externalities are market-registered actions that benefit some people and hurt others, and may not result in a net gain or loss to society. Policy interventions to counteract a pecuniary externality imply a value judgment favoring redistribution of income from one group to another. For instance, a farmer's decision to plant an extra acre of wheat will slightly depress the market price of wheat. Although the price decrement is minute, it affects the entire crop so that the total loss of income to other farmers is a palpable amount. This loss to farmers, however, is a gain to consumers. Policies that restrict agricultural acreage or crop production, which are often found in developed countries, represent a political determination to redistribute income from consumers to farmers.

A decision to bear children can impose both true and pecuniary externalities on other members of society. In this chapter we consider the conclusions of some previous chapters to determine the role of externalities in private childbearing decisions. We discuss three situations in which private fertility decisions have social repercussions: in the use of common-property resources, in the labor market, and in the intrafamily allocation of goods. The chapter concludes with a discussion of policy implications and options.

COMMON-PROPERTY RESOURCES AND PUBLICLY SUBSIDIZED GOODS AND SERVICES

As discussed under Question 3, population growth can exacerbate the externalities inherent in common-property resources. Resources for which well-defined rights of access either do not exist or are not enforced are typically overexploited and subject to damage. These include environmental resources like air and water, some forests and fisheries, and some agricultural land. While the cause of problems is the absence of limits on use, the demand for many common-property resources increases with population growth, particularly those resources required for food production or related to human settlement. If population growth contributes to long-run resource degradation or destruction, the cost falls on the society as a whole, not just on those making childbearing decisions.

A related external effect involves the public sector provision of infrastructure. All governments assume responsibility for providing certain public goods that the private sector is unable to provide because of the difficulty of charging users, the large investments required, or the inefficiency of excluding potential users. Such goods include transportation systems, sanitation and water supply, and national defense.

Population growth can have a beneficial effect on the provision of public goods by permitting the exploitation of economies of scale to reduce per capita costs. However, economies of scale in the production of most public infrastructure tend to diminish as the size of the population to be served increases (Henderson, 1985), so that population growth beyond certain levels confers no additional benefit. Moreover, rapid population growth in developing countries, particularly in urban areas, contributes to congestion and excessive demands on existing infrastructures (Linn, 1983) and may promote disease transmission. Because these congestion costs must be borne by the society as a whole, not just by the families who bear many children, rapid population growth may have net negative external effects on public welfare.

The logic supporting publicly subsidized education is usually of a different sort, stressing the social interest in having a well-educated electorate and labor force or the importance of supplying a population's basic needs. Nevertheless, public education also creates externalities. Publicly subsidized education disproportionately benefits families with children, at least in the short run, and a couple's decision to have an extra child imposes costs on all taxpayers. Some of these costs will be reimbursed by future tax payments by the educated child to support the education of other people's children. Given the high rates of return to social investment in schooling that we noted above, the added taxes paid by an additional educated adult may be substantial. But the present value of those future tax payments may be less than current educational costs. Moreover, both families and governments typically find it difficult to finance current educational costs by borrowing against future earnings. Thus, the birth of an additional child into a society that offers subsidized education would impose external costs. Subsidies for the aged work in the opposite direction. In a society that offered tax-financed social security benefits (but not public education), the birth of an additional child would confer external benefits, and fertility would fall below the socially optimal level (Willis, 1985).

WAGES AND RENTS

In answering Question 4, we concluded that more rapid population growth can tend to depress wages and raise the return to capital and land. Hence, it is clear that childbearing decisions result, at the least, in pecuniary externalities. Population growth among the co-owners of a common resource will, of course, dilute each owner's share of the resource. In general, families with relatively large amounts of capital or land are advantaged by other families' high fertility, while families that rely primarily on labor income are disadvantaged.

A much more difficult question is whether true externalities also exist in a competitive market of self-interested families. In other words, does higher fertility result not merely in a redistribution from workers to landowners, but in a net loss of welfare to society as a whole? This line of research is comparatively new and still entirely theoretical in nature. Preliminary results (Nerlove et al., 1984; Willis, 1985) indicate that under certain restrictive assumptions–such as a population of identical individuals–there are no true externalities, but that if some of those assumptions are relaxed–for instance, if the population is heterogeneous–there may be true externalities. However, it is clear that true externalities do exist if individuals care not only about their own families, but about the extent of poverty or the degree of income inequality in the society. An increase in fertility will, at least in the short run, shift income from landless workers to owners of land and capital. This shift will tend to increase both the number of people who are poor (defined in absolute income terms) and the degree of income inequality in the society. To the extent that these results are believed by the society to be undesirable, there is a social rationale for restricting fertility, similar to the rationale for land redistribution.

INTRAFAMILY EXTERNALITIES

If parents do not behave altruistically out of concern for the welfare of their children, intergenerational externalities will exist even within the same family line. Parental altruism is an intuitively appealing premise, since family behavior interpretable in this manner seems pervasive across cultures. Indeed, one can argue that altruistic family behavioral norms reflect the importance of intergenerational cooperation, representing a nonmarket social institution that serves to internalize potential external effects. And, in a stable culture, it is not unreasonable to expect that family size norms embody reliable information about the economic conditions that will be faced by the next generation. The near-universality of parental altruism and its ability to compensate for intergenerational external effects probably explains why reproductive rights are ceded to the family in almost all societies, even though population size has important collective consequences.

Of course, parental altruism can fail. Parents may decide to have children in order to exploit them economically with no concern for their well-being. Similarly, parents may abuse or neglect children. Many societies have laws that seek to protect children from exploitation, abuse, or neglect by adults, suggesting that family sovereignty is not always considered an immutable principle. But even if parents make fertility decisions that try to take the future well-being of children into account, their expectations may not be realized. Because of the scope and speed of the social and economic changes that characterize developing countries, families may be unable to correctly anticipate the impact on the family of an additional child.

If existing children are disadvantaged by a subsequent birth in the family, then one can ask whether there is a legitimate role for government intervention to represent the interests of those children in parents' childbearing decisions. Such interventions have precedents in child labor laws and compulsory school legislation. If this basis for social intervention is accepted, then the justification for government programs related to fertility becomes much broader than if externalities are confined to interfamily relations. Similar questions could also be raised about relations between husband and wife. These questions involve major issues about the proper basis for social decision making and, ultimately, about values–issues that lie well beyond our competence.

POLICY IMPLICATIONS OF POPULATION EXTERNALITIES

Under Question 6 and again in the conclusion of this report, we argue that the provision of family planning services increases parents' welfare by allowing them to achieve the number and spacing of births they desire. Thus family planning programs have a solid rationale on the basis of within-family effects. Where negative externalities from childbearing exist, the voluntary use of family planning services by one family confers external benefits on others, making family planning a particularly attractive policy instrument.

But the existence of negative externalities implies that even if all parents achieve their desired family size, the number of births may still be above the social optimum. A case can then be made for policies "beyond family planning." It must be recognized immediately that any policy entails some cost–at a minimum, an administrative cost–and that the case for such policies can only be made by comparing costs to benefits. Policies that go beyond family planning may also impose welfare costs and require families to forgo the satisfaction from additional children.

Principles of welfare economics suggest that one should distinguish among three kinds of policies: those that alter childbearing incentives via taxes or subsidies, those that change "tastes" for children, and those that impose fixed limits on the number of children per family. We first compare the first and last kinds of policies, then consider the second.

If the other costs of a given fertility reduction are equal, the last policy is the least attractive because it will lead to a substantial welfare loss for those people who place a high value on bearing an additional child but who are prevented from doing so. Furthermore, the means of enforcing quantity rationing are almost certain to be coercive, impinging on personal liberties in the very sensitive area of reproductive rights. Compared with quantity rationing, an advantage of altering incentive structures by a system of subsidies or taxes is that the people who choose to reduce their fertility in response to a rise in the "cost" of children are likely to place the lowest value on having an additional child. This favorable selectivity feature suggests that the private welfare loss to childbearing couples from a reduction in fertility will be less when incentive schemes are used than when quantity rationing is imposed. Another clear advantage for incentive schemes is that childbearing remains purely voluntary. One must, of course, be aware of other effects of policy, such as their impact on different social groups and the potential for abuses in their implementation.

The advantage of incentive schemes becomes less clear-cut when children's welfare is introduced. Many policies that would work by raising the relative costs of children (e.g., reducing subsidies for schooling, lowering tax deductions for children) have the effect of redistributing income from families that have children and may thereby compromise other social goals. Other forms of incentive programs, which avoid this effect, include incentives to delay marriage, to space births further apart, or to use various forms of contraception. Less direct actions include providing old-age support for persons without children. Governmentally imposed incentives that affect many forms of personal behavior are common in many societies, and incentive programs to alter fertility do not appear different in nature from most of them.

A comparison of incentives and coercion also introduces equity issues, similar to those related to a comparison of a volunteer and a universal (a lottery-based) draft. In short, poorer people tend to find the incentives more attractive than richer people, who may, in effect, disproportionately "buy out" of the incentive scheme to restrict births. So the favorable effect of an incentive program on the distribution of income may be partly offset by unfavorable effects on the distribution of children by class. Nevertheless, the voluntary nature of incentives programs at least has the advantage that the outcome for a particular family is freely chosen.

Government programs designed to change "tastes" for children are difficult to evaluate from the viewpoint of welfare economics, which takes tastes as a given. But it is clear that a change in preference for children relative to market goods, which leads to altered fertility, might resolve problems of external effects related to population growth. However, programs designed to effect that change pose some potential problems. Persuasion campaigns in the mass media can shade into propaganda that involves deception and misinformation. Unless they are done with sensitivity, they can stigmatize children as well as adults who choose to have them. One could, however, take the position that such campaigns are simply designed to counteract pronatalist norms and customs developed under earlier conditions. In most populations, powerful norms governing family behavior are pronatalist because a major function of the family has been to ensure reproduction of both itself and the society of which it is a part.

Other kinds of policy changes fit less readily into the categories of welfare economics. Mandated changes–often adaptive–in the status of women, greater emphasis on rural development, and many other development programs basically involve changes in the structure of society and can be expected to have some effect on fertility (for a discussion of these issues, see Ridker, 1976; Schutjer and Stokes, 1984; Bulatao, 1984). Besides advancing other social goals, such programs affect fertility either through changes in incentives or changes in tastes, rather than through quantity rationing.

CONCLUSIONS

Private fertility decisions have several external effects. First, where there are common-property resources, population growth can result in congestion or over-rapid resource degradation. Second, publicly subsidized entitlements to education or social security can cause childbearing to have either external costs or benefits, depending on the tax system, the discount rate, and a child's prospective lifetime income profile. Similarly, the provision of public infrastructure can result in either negative or positive externalities, depending on whether the infrastructure is subject to congestion or to economies of scale. Third, population growth tends to benefit holders of land and capital and hurt those who depend primarily on wages for income. Fourth, parental fertility decisions may not always be in their children's best interests, particularly when parents underestimate the pace and consequences of social change over their children's lifetimes.

These effects are likely to result in a negative external effect of childbearing in most developing countries, where there are no social security systems and where economies of scale in infrastructure are more than counterbalanced by congestion costs. When negative externalities exist, a minimum policy prescription would include the subsidized provision of family planning services to allow couples to achieve their desired levels of fertility. Reducing the number of unwanted births in a given family results both in direct welfare gains to the family and in gains to society at large. To fully overcome the negative externalities, however, would require additional policy action. If the external effects are deemed sizable enough to warrant policy intervention, alterations in incentive structures appear far more appealing from the viewpoint of welfare economics than does quantity rationing. It is important to note, however, that current data and theory are inadequate to quantify the size of external effects; certainly, there is no evidence to suggest that drastic financial or legal restrictions on childbearing are warranted.

Conclusion

We have examined a diverse set of mechanisms through which population growth affects economic development. This chapter opens with a review and synthesis of our conclusions on the expected effects of a decline in the population growth rate that works through these mechanisms. It then proceeds to a discussion of how environmental and institutional contexts mediate the actions of these mechanisms–a major theme of this report. The final section discusses policy implications.

EFFECTS OF SLOWER POPULATION GROWTH ON ECONOMIC DEVELOPMENT

Following the framework set up in the Introduction, we consider how conditions are likely to differ if a country, through a government program, were to achieve and maintain lower fertility than it would otherwise have experienced (with constant mortality). As noted above, such a decline would produce at every subsequent point slower population growth, smaller population size, lower population density, and an older age structure. Working through these direct demographic effects, a reduced level of fertility is also likely to produce several other changes.

Slower Population Growth and Exhaustible Resources

Globally slower population growth may delay the time at which a particular stage of depletion of an exhaustible resource is reached. This effect does not necessarily increase the number of people who will have access to

85

that resource; rather, it moves the consumption stream further from the present. But it is important to recognize that no single exhaustible resource is essential or irreplaceable; it is valued for its economic contribution, not for its own sake. As easily accessible reserves of natural resources are exhausted, the real cost of extraction, and hence the resource price, rises. This price rise should stimulate the search for alternative materials. Historically, these adaptive strategies have been extremely successful. To the extent that slower population growth results in a slower rate of resource depletion, these adaptive strategies will also occur more slowly. Hence, it seems unlikely that slower population growth will allow a larger number of people, over future generations, to enjoy a given standard of living thanks to lower natural resource prices.

Slower Population Growth and Renewable Resources

Slower population growth, in some cases nationally and in others globally, is likely to lead to a reduced rate of degradation of renewable common-property resources such as air, water, and species of plants and animals. If significant amounts of land and forest resources are held in common in a country, they will also tend to be degraded less rapidly. These effects are likely to be more evident in the short run–in say, a decade or two. In the long run, population growth itself might create greater incentives to develop the social and political institutions necessary for conservation. Such incentives are irrelevant, of course, if the resource has become depleted beyond the point of restoration. Moreover, changes are costly and the need to bear such costs is itself a consequence of population growth.

Slower Population Growth, Health, and Education

Lower fertility is likely to raise average per child levels of household expenditure on health and education and thereby improve levels of child health and education. By themselves, such changes should result in a more productive labor force. Superimposed on these within-family effects is the possibility that lower fertility will alter the distribution of children among families by income class. If fertility declines are largest among high-income families, average levels of schooling and health among children could actually decrease despite an absolute improvement in measures of well-being among poor families. But if family planning programs result in larger fertility reductions among poorer families, the within-family gains will be accentuated at the societal level.

Slower population growth is likely to raise public expenditures on schooling per school-aged child. Evidence from the educational literature suggests that such a result may lead to some improvement in educational quality as measured, for example, by test scores. We do not find convincing evidence that lower fertility will result in faster growth in enrollment ratios (apart from within-family effects).

Slower Population Growth and Income

Unless a fertility decline is concentrated among high-income families, it is likely to lead to a reduction in income disparities among social classes. This is primarily a long-term effect (although a variety of short-term effects are also possible) and works primarily by raising payments to labor relative to payments to capital and raising payments to unskilled labor relative to skilled labor.

We have found little evidence that the aggregate savings rate depends on growth rates or the age structure of a population. Assuming that the savings rate remains unchanged, a fertility decline will lead to an increase in the ratio of capital to labor and, along with it, labor productivity, wages, and per capita income. The increase in the capital/labor ratio will reduce rates of return to capital and reduce payments to owners of capital.

In the short run, more land per agricultural worker is likely to raise labor productivity in agriculture. Long-term effects may differ because of changes in the organization and techniques of production that are induced by the relative change in factor availability. These effects may reduce the short-term gains of slower growth.

Slower Population Growth and Cities

With slower population growth, cities grow more slowly, both in the short and long run. Natural increase (the excess of births over deaths) accounts for about 60 percent of city growth today in developing countries, and it is reasonable to expect that a decline in fertility levels will entail a decline in rates of natural increase in cities. Such changes reduce the demand for urban infrastructural investments while eventually reducing the revenue base that supports such investments. The evidence on whether reduced national fertility levels reduce the rate of rural-urban migration, and hence reduce the rate of growth of the proportion of the population that is urban, is unclear.

A reduced rate of urban labor force growth in developing countries (most of which is a product of natural increase among the urban population) is not likely to be systematically accompanied by corresponding reductions in joblessness. However, it may increase the proportion of the urban labor force working in high-wage jobs in the modern sector of the economy and reduce the proportion working in the low-wage, informal sector.

ENVIRONMENTAL AND INSTITUTIONAL CONTEXTS

It is clear that the economic advantages of fertility reduction will vary from place to place. Environmental and climatic conditions clearly shape the local impact of population growth. In countries such as Bangladesh, where ratios of agricultural labor to arable land are already very high, there is a presumptive case that labor productivity in agriculture will decline more rapidly with added labor than if ratios were low. Nonagricultural production possibilities, and the opportunities for trade, also affect the importance of these natural features.

Important as these natural features may be in conditioning the economic response to population growth, they appear to be far less important than conditions created by people. Many of the initial effects of population growth are negative, but they can be ameliorated or even reversed in the long run if institutional adjustment mechanisms are in place. Among the most important of such mechanisms are property rights in land and properly functioning markets for labor, capital, and goods. Such markets permit the initial effects of population growth to be registered in the form of price changes, which can trigger a variety of adjustments, including the introduction of other factors of production that have become more valuable as a result of the increase in population; a search for substitutes for increasingly scarce factors of production; intensified research to find production processes better suited to the new conditions; reallocation of resources toward sectors (e.g., food production) in which demand may be most responsive to population change; and so on. Of course, these adjustments may entail real costs, even when these are minimized by efficient institutions. When markets function very poorly, or do not exist, adjustments to population change are likely to be slower or to not occur at all. These are not merely theoretical notions. Some part of the current distress in Ethiopia, of the loss of 30 million lives during China's "great leap forward" (Ashton et al., 1984), and of the problems of food production in tropical Africa during the 1970s was due to very badly functioning markets combined with rapid population growth.

Even efficient markets do not guarantee desirable outcomes. The famines of 1942-1943 in Bengal and of 1973-1974 in Bangladesh seem to have been principally a result of deterioration in the income distribution—in particular, the loss of purchasing power by unskilled wage laborers—combined with speculative hoarding in food markets (Sen, 1981). This kind of outcome underscores the role of the distribution of wealth and of human capital as a fundamental determinant of poverty.

The potential value of government intervention for market regulation and for purposes of income distribution is widely acknowledged. Government policies in a variety of arenas clearly play important roles in mediating the impact of population growth. Effects of population growth on educational enrollment and quality, on rates of exploitation of common property resources, on the development of social and economic infrastructure, on urbanization, and on research activities are all heavily dependent on existing government policies and their adaptiveness to changed conditions.

In short, the effects of rapid population growth are likely to be conditioned by the quality of markets, the nature of government policies, and features of the natural environment. Since the effects are so dependent on these conditions, a reliable assessment of many of the net effects of population growth can best be carried out at the national level, although some issues concerning the environment and resources can only be analyzed globally.

It is of interest to briefly examine and contrast the interplay between population growth and institutions in two important areas, China and tropical Africa. China, with its extremely low arable land/population ratio, is often seen as greatly in need of population control policies in order to boost per capita agricultural income; this view is reflected in the government's severe disincentives for large families. Although it is possible that the resultant decline in the population growth rate has somewhat increased per capita agricultural income, these gains are probably small compared with those from agricultural reforms instituted in 1979. Over the period 1979-1984, the real per capita income of the rural population increased 15 percent annually, and total agricultural output increased 51 percent (U.S. Department of Agriculture, 1985; Li, 1985).

In contrast, tropical Africa has a comparatively high land/population ratio, but appears to be particularly vulnerable to problems induced by population growth. Political independence and the forces of modernization came to tropical Africa later than to other areas. Although some countries in other regions also share these traits, markets are generally least well developed in tropical Africa, political factionalism is greatest, and human resource potential is least developed. In parts of Africa, sparseness of population itself may be responsible for some of these difficulties, but this explanation is implausible for such countries as Ethiopia or Kenya. Obviously, slowing population growth is not a substitute for solving other problems, but it can reduce some of the more extreme manifestations of these problems while they are being solved.

SUMMARY

Population growth can, and often does, trigger market reactions. Many of these reactions move a country in a "modern" direction, that is, toward better-defined property rights, larger integrated markets, more agricultural research, and so on. However, the market-induced adjustments to higher growth do not appear to be large enough to offset the negative effects on per capita income of higher ratios of labor to other factors of production. Nor is population growth necessary to achieve these forms of modernization: the fact that rates of return to agricultural research are already extremely high–in both developing and developed countries–implies that there is little need for additional stimulus from population growth; the evolution of property rights is stimulated by many factors–population growth being only one among them (Binswanger and Pingali, 1984); and the scope of many markets can be enlarged by removing trade barriers. That these other devices exist does not imply a minimal role for population growth, but it does caution against advocacy of growth as the only way to achieve them.

On balance, we reach the qualitative conclusion that slower population growth would be beneficial to economic development for most developing countries. A rigorous quantitative assessment of these benefits is difficult and context dependent. Since we have stressed the role of slower population growth in raising per capita human and physical capital, it is instructive to use as a benchmark the effects of changes in the ratio of physical capital per person. A simple model suggests that the effect is comparatively modest. Using a typical labor coefficient of 0.5 in estimated production functions, a 1 percent reduction in the rate of labor force growth would boost the growth of per capita income by 0.5 percent per year. Thus, after 30 years, a 1 percent reduction in the annual rate of population growth (produced, say, by a decline in the crude birth rate from 37 to 27 per 1,000) will have raised production and income per capita to a level 16 percent above what it would otherwise have been. This would be a substantial gain, but by no means enough to vault a typical developing country into the ranks of the developed.

This simple calculation, however, does not fully reflect the complexity of the linkages between population growth and economic development. For instance, the production function would be expected to change in ways that reduce the advantages of slower population growth. We have reviewed considerable evidence, particularly in the agricultural sector, of how technology adapts to changes in factor proportions. In most places it is reasonable to expect slower growth in the labor force to reduce the intensity of adaptive response in the form of land improvement, irrigation, and agricultural research. On the other hand, the calculation does not reflect increases in production due to the healthier and better educated work force that would result from lower fertility.

Much more sophisticated models of production and fertility have been constructed with a variety of assumptions about the nature and intensity of relationships between economic and demographic variables (see Ahlburg, 1985, for a thorough review). None of these models embodies the more recent evidence on the nature and magnitude of effects that is included here, and we are not in a position to endorse any of the models.

Careful scientific research is needed both to better quantify and to further elucidate most of the relationships discussed in this book. Research is especially needed on urbanization and the consequences of urban growth; savings and the formation of physical capital; the effect of population growth on health, education, and the development of human capital; and the nature and extent of externalities of childbearing. Such research would be appropriately supported by mission-oriented development organizations as well as by basic research agencies.

Whether the economic problems posed by population growth are large or small, and whether they are best approached by slowing the population growth rate, depends ultimately on the costs of alternative policy responses. We now turn to outline those responses.

POLICY IMPLICATIONS: THE ROLE OF FAMILY PLANNING

We have stressed that population growth can exacerbate the ill effects of a variety of inefficient policies, such as urban bias in the provision of infrastructure, direct and indirect food subsidies that distort agricultural markets, credit market distortions, and inadequate management of common property. A fundamental solution to these problems lies in better policies outside the population arena. However, some policies may be extremely resistant to correction, even over the medium to long term. Moreover, we have found some beneficial effects of slower population growth even in the presence of well-functioning markets and other institutions. Thus, there appears to be a legitimate role for population policy, providing its benefits exceed its costs.

Although educational and health policies may have indirect effects on fertility, family planning programs have been the most conventional and direct instrument of government population policy. By family planning programs, we mean the provision of contraceptive services, together with information about contraception and child spacing. The total amount spent on family planning programs in 1982 was less than $2 billion, of which international assistance represents about $330 million (World Bank, 1984:148). By comparison, total official development assistance by Organization for Economic Cooperation and Development (OECD) countries was about $27.5 billion in 1983 (World Bank, 1984:252). In most developing countries, family planning program expenditures represent less than 1 percent of the government budget.

Government support for family planning programs can have an economic and social rationale quite apart from the effect of programs on rates of population growth. In many societies, individual control of reproduction is considered a basic human right, similar in nature to good health or literacy. Lack of information about reproduction services and other services may constrain parents from achieving their desired number and spacing of children. In such a situation, the supply of information and services will increase family welfare. Governments can often supply information and services about reproduction more efficiently and cheaply than the private sector, in part because large and risky investments are required and because some of the benefits to consumers cannot be captured by the suppliers. In particular, valuable information can flow from person to person without any financial reward to the initial supplier: information about the consequences of childbearing is one example; the rhythm method is another. In this case, the private sector will underinvest in the provision of such services. The rationale for government support for family planning programs is similar to that for support of a variety of public health programs, as well as for agricultural research and extension services. Furthermore, when health services are provided by government, an additional rationale for government family planning programs is that the services can be efficiently supplied by existing health personnel (World Bank, 1984). Finally, family planning programs are likely to be of more value to lower income groups than to higher income groups, who may have better access to private services, so government support for these programs can help to advance equity goals.

If people use the services and information supplied by government family planning programs and if fertility falls as a result, an obvious case can be made that the program has increased the private welfare of users by reducing the cost of fertility control and by reducing the gap between desired and achieved fertility. This gain in private well-being is added to whatever other gains accrue on the national agenda from fertility reduction. The large fertility declines that occurred in such countries as Mexico, Indonesia, and Thailand during the 1970s–declines that were associated over time with intensified national family planning programs–suggest that private welfare gains from such programs are large. The large amount of unwanted childbearing in developing countries that was revealed by the World Fertility Survey (Boulier, 1985) suggests that such programs have considerable remaining potential to increase private welfare and reduce population growth rates.

When national economic and social goals can be furthered by a reduction in fertility, the fact that family planning programs can achieve such reductions while increasing the well-being of users of these services accounts for much of their attractiveness as a policy instrument for governments in developing countries. A similar attractiveness applies to removal of legal prohibitions against access to means of fertility control, prohibitions that pose serious obstacles to couples' reproductive behavior in many countries (Berelson and Lieberson, 1979). In sum, there is little debate about the desirability of programs that allow couples access to easy, affordable, and effective means of family planning, even among those who see population growth as a neutral or even a positive influence on development (Wattenberg and Zinsmeister, 1985).

When a couple's childbearing decision imposes external costs on other families–in overexploitation of common resources, congestion of public services, or contribution to a socially undesirable distribution of income– a case may be made for policies that go "beyond family planning." Such policies include persuasive campaigns to change family size norms and combinations of incentives and taxes related to family size. It is more difficult to make the case for the imposition of drastic financial or legal restrictions on childbearing. As noted above, such restrictions are likely to entail large welfare losses at the individual level; these losses would be hard to assess quantitatively, as are the possible social benefits of such restrictions.

Because economic development is a multifaceted process, no single policy or single-sector strategy can be successful by itself. Thus, family planning programs by themselves cannot make a poor country rich or even move it many notches higher on the scale of development. However, family planning programs that enable couples to have the number of children they desire increase the private welfare of the people who use their services while reducing the burden on society of whatever economic externalities exist. And family planning programs are likely to increase the well-being of the users' children and to extend rather than to restrict personal choices. Thus, family planning programs can play a role in improving the lives of people in developing countries.

References

Ahlburg, D.A. (1985) The Impact of Population Growth on Economic Growth in Developing Nations: The Evidence from Macroeconomic-Demographic Models. Background paper prepared for the Working Group on Population Growth and Economic Development, Committee on Population, National Research Council, Washington, D.C.

Allan, W. (1965) *The African Husbandman*. London: Oliver and Boyd.

Arthur, W.B., and G. McNicoll (1978) Samuelson, population and intergenerational transfers. *International Economic Review* 19(1):241-246.

Ashton, B., K. Hill, A. Piazza, and R. Zeitz (1984) Famine in China, 1958-61. *Population and Development Review* 10(4):613-646.

Bale, M., and R. Duncan (1983) Food prospects in the developing countries: a qualified optimistic view. *American Economic Review* 73:244-248.

Barlow, R. (1967) The economic effects of malaria eradication. *American Economic Review* 57:130-157.

Barlow, R. (1979) Health and economic development: a theoretical and empirical review. *Research in Human Capital and Development* 1:45-75.

Barnett, H.J., G.M. van Muiswinkel, M. Schechter, and J.J. Myers (1984) The global trends in nonfuel minerals. Pp. 316-338 in J.L. Simon and H. Kahn, eds., *The Resourceful Earth: A Response to Global 2000*. New York: Basil Blackwell.

Baumol, W., and W. Oates (1984) Long-run trends in environmental quality. In J.L. Simon and H. Kahn, eds., *The Resourceful Earth: A Response to Global 2000*. New York: Basil Blackwell.

Beckford, G.L. (1984) Induced innovation model of agricultural development: comment. Pp. 75-81 in C.K. Eicher and J. Staatz, eds., *Agricultural Development in the Third World*. Baltimore, Md.: Johns Hopkins University Press.

Beckmann, P. (1984) Solar energy and other "alternative" energy. In J.L. Simon and H. Kahn, eds., *The Resourceful Earth: A Response to Global 2000*. New York: Basil Blackwell.

Behrman, J.R., and N. Birdsall (1983) The quality of schooling: quantity alone is misleading. *American Economic Review* 73:928-946.

94

Behrman, J.R., and N. Birdsall (1985) The Reward for Choosing Well the Timing of One's Birth: Cohort Effects and Earnings Functions for Brazilian Males. World Bank, Washington, D.C.

Berelson, B. (1975) *The Great Debate on Population Policy: An Instructive Entertainment.* New York: The Population Council.

Berelson, B., and J. Lieberson (1979) Government efforts to influence fertility: the ethical issues. *Population and Development Review* 5(4):581-613.

Binswanger, H.P., and P.L. Pingali (1984) The Evolution of Farming Systems and Agricultural Technology in Sub-Saharan Africa. Discussion Paper ARU-23. World Bank, Washington, D.C.

Birdsall, N. (1977) Analytical approaches to the relationship of population growth and development. *Population and Development Review* 3(1-2):63-102.

Birdsall, N. (1980) The cost of siblings: child schooling in urban Colombia. *Research in Population Economics* 2:115-150.

Boserup, E. (1965) *The Conditions of Agricultural Growth.* Chicago: Aldine Publishing Co.

Boserup, E. (1981) *Population and Technological Change.* Chicago: University of Chicago Press.

Boulier, B.L. (1985) Evaluating Unmet Needs for Contraception: Estimates for Thirty-Six Developing Countries. Working Paper No. 678. World Bank, Washington, D.C.

Brackett, J.W. (1978) Family planning in four Latin American countries—knowledge, use and unmet needs: some findings from the World Fertility Survey. *International Family Planning Perspectives* 4(4):116-123.

Breman, H., and C.T. de Wit (1983) Rangeland productivity and exploitation in the Sahel. *Science* 221:1341-1347.

Brown, L.R. (1981) World population growth, soil erosion, and food security. *Science* 214:995-1001.

Brown, L.R. (1984) Securing food supplies. Pp. 175-193 in L.R. Brown et al., eds., *State of the World.* New York: W.W. Norton & Co.

Bulatao, R. (1979) On the Nature of the Transition in the Value of Children. Paper No. 60-A. The East-West Population Institute, Honolulu, Hawaii.

Bulatao, R. (1984) Reducing Fertility in Developing Countries: A Review of Determinants and Policy Levers. Working Paper No. 680. World Bank, Washington, D.C.

Bureau of the Census (1983) *World Population 1983–Recent Demographic Estimates for the Countries and Regions of the World.* Washington, D.C.: U.S. Department of Commerce.

Cain, M. (1983) Fertility as an adjustment to risk. *Population and Development Review* 9(4):688-702.

Caldwell, J.C., P.H. Reddy, and P. Caldwell (1982) Demographic change in rural south India. *Population and Development Review* 8:680-727.

Chandler, W. (1984) Recycling materials. Pp. 95-114 in L.R. Brown et al., eds., *State of the World.* New York: W.W. Norton & Co.

Chenery, H., and M. Syrquin (1975) *Patterns of Development, 1950-1970.* New York: Oxford University Press.

Clark, C. (1978) *Mathematical Bioeconomics: The Optimal Management of Renewable Resources.* New York: Wiley.

Clawson, M. (1982) Private forests. Pp. 283-292 in P.R. Portney and R.B. Hass, eds., *Current Issues in Natural Resources Policy.* Baltimore, Md.: Johns Hopkins University Press.

Coale, A.J. (1978) Population growth and economic development: the case of Mexico. *Foreign Affairs* 56(2):415-429.

Coale, A.J. (1984) *Rapid Population Change in China*, 1952-1982. Washington, D.C: National Academy Press.

Coale, A.J., and E.M. Hoover (1958) *Population Growth and Economic Development in Low-Income Countries.* Princeton, N.J.: Princeton University Press.

Cochrane, S.H. (1983) Development Consequences of Rapid Population Growth: A Review from the Perspective of Sub-Sahara Africa. Background paper for Report on Population Strategies for Sub-Saharan Africa. World Bank, Washington, D.C.

Commoner, B., M. Carr, and P.J. Stamler (1971) The causes of pollution. *Environment* 13(3):2-19.

Corsa, L., Jr., and D. Oakley (1971) Consequences of population growth for health services in less developed countries–an initial appraisal. Pp. 368-402 in National Academy of Sciences, *Rapid Population Growth: Consequences and Policy Implications,* Vol. II. Baltimore, Md.: Johns Hopkins University Press.

Council on Environmental Quality and U.S. Department of State (1980) *The Global 2000 Report to the President.* Washington, D.C.: U.S. Government Printing Office.

Crosson, P.R. (1982) Agricultural land. Pp. 253-282 in P.R. Portney and R.B. Hass, eds., *Current Issues in Natural Resources Policy.* Baltimore, Md.: Johns Hopkins University Press.

Crosson, P.R. (1983) Soil Erosion in Developing Countries: Amounts, Consequences, and Policies. Working Paper No. 21. Center for Resource Policy Studies, School of Natural Resources, University of Wisconsin, Madison.

Crosson, P.R. (1984) National Costs of Erosion Effects on Productivity. Unpublished paper. Resources for the Future, Washington, D.C.

Dasgupta, P. (1985) The Ethical Foundations of Population Policy. Background paper prepared for the Working Group on Population Growth and Economic Development, Committee on Population, National Research Council, Washington, D.C.

Dasgupta, P., and G.M. Heal (1979) *Economic Theory and Exhaustible Resources.* Cambridge, England: Cambridge University Press.

David, P. (1975) *Technical Choice, Innovation and Economic Growth.* Cambridge, England: Cambridge University Press.

Deardorff, A.V. (1985) Trade and Capital Mobility in a World of Diverging Populations. Background paper prepared for the Working Group on Population Growth and Economic Development, Committee on Population, National Research Council, Washington, D.C.

Deevey, E.S., D. Rice, P. Rice, H.H. Vaughan, M. Brenner, and M.S. Flannery (1979) Mayan urbanism: impact on a tropical karst environment. *Science* 206(19):198-306.

de Janvry, E. (1984) The political economy of rural development in Latin America: an interpretation. Pp. 82-95 in C.K. Eicher and J. Staatz, eds., *Agricultural Development in the Third World.* Baltimore, Md.: Johns Hopkins University Press.

Denison, E.F. (1962) *The Sources of Economic Growth and the Alternatives Before Us.* New York: Committee for Economic Development.

Denison, E.F. (1974) *Accounting for United States Economic Growth, 1929-1969.* Washington, D.C.: Brookings Institution.

Denison, E.F., and W.K. Chung (1976) *How Japan's Economy Grew So Fast.* Washington, D.C.: Brookings Institution.

Deolalikar, A. (1984) Are There Primary Returns to Health in Agricultural Work? An Econometric Analysis of Agricultural Wages and Farm Productivity in Rural South India. Unpublished manuscript. Department of Economics, University of Pennsylvania.

Easterlin, R.E., ed. (1980) *Population and Economic Change in Developing Countries.* Chicago: University of Chicago Press.

Economic Commission for Africa (1984) Food production and population in Africa. Pp. 241-266 in United Nations International Conference on Population, *Population, Resources, Environment, and Development.* Population Study No. 90, ST/ESA/SER.A/90. New York: United Nations.

Eicher, C.K. (1984) Facing up to Africa's food crisis. Pp. 452-480 in C.K. Eicher and J. Staatz, eds., *Agricultural Development in the Third World*. Baltimore, Md.: Johns Hopkins University Press.

Eicher, C.K., and J. Staatz, eds. (1984) *Agricultural Development in the Third World*. Baltimore, Md.: Johns Hopkins University Press.

Ernst, C., and J. Angst (1983) *Birth Order: Its Influence on Personality*. New York: Springer-Verlag.

Evenson, R.E. (1984a) Benefits and obstacles in developing appropriate agricultural technology. Pp. 348-361 in C.K. Eicher and J. Staatz, eds., *Agricultural Development in the Third World*. Baltimore, Md.: Johns Hopkins University Press.

Evenson, R.E. (1984b) Population Growth, Infrastructural Development, Technology and Welfare in Rural North India. Paper prepared for the IUSSP Seminar on Population and Rural Development. New Delhi, India.

Fields, G. (1975) Rural-urban migration, urban unemployment and underemployment, and job search activity in LDCs. *Journal of Development Economics* 2:165-187.

Firor, J.W., and P.R. Portney (1982) The world climate. Pp. 179-215 in P.R. Portney, ed., *Current Issues in Natural Resources Policy*. Washington, D.C.: Resources for the Future.

Flavin, C., and S. Postel (1984) Developing renewable energy. Pp. 136-174 in L.R. Brown et al., eds., *State of the World 1984*. New York: W.W. Norton & Co.

Food and Agriculture Organization (1981) *Agriculture: Toward 2000*. Rome: Food and Agriculture Organization.

Food and Agriculture Organization (1983) Land, Food, and Population. FAO Conference Session 22, 5 November 1983, Rome, Italy.

Ghatak, S., and K. Ingersent (1984) *Agriculture and Economic Development*. Baltimore, Md.: Johns Hopkins University Press.

Gilbert, A. (1976) The argument for very large cities reconsidered. *Urban Studies* 13(1):27-34.

Giovannini, A. (1983) Interest-elasticity of savings in developing countries: the existing evidence. *World Development* 11(7):601-607.

Glover, D., and J.L. Simon (1975) The effects of population density on infrastructure: the case of road building. *Economic Development and Cultural Change* 23:453-468.

Goeller, H.E., and A. Zucker (1984) Infinite resources: the ultimate strategy. *Science* 223:456-462.

Golladay, F., and B. Liese (1980) Health Issues and Policies in the Developing World. Working Paper No. 412. World Bank, Washington, D.C.

Gould, J. (1972) *Economic Growth in History: Survey and Analysis*. London: Methuen & Company.

Gourou, P. (1980) *The Tropical World: Its Social and Economic Conditions and Its Future Status*, 5th edition. New York: Longman.

Greenwood, M.J. (1969) The determinants of labor migration in Egypt. *Journal of Regional Science* 9:283-290.

Greenwood, M.J. (1971) Regression analysis of migration to urban areas of a less-developed country: the case of India. *Journal of Regional Science* 11:253-262.

Greenwood, M.J. (1978) An econometric model of internal migration and regional economic growth in Mexico. *Journal of Regional Science* 18:17-31.

Gregory, P. (1980) An assessment of changes in employment conditions in less developed countries. *Economic Development and Cultural Change* 28(4):673-700.

Habakkuk, H.J. (1962) *American and British Technology in the Nineteenth Century*. Cambridge, England: Cambridge University Press.

Hammer, J.S. (1984) Population Growth and Savings in Less Developed Countries. Background paper prepared for the *1984 World Development Report*. World Bank, Washington, D.C.

Hanushek, E.A. (1981) Throwing money at schools. *Journal of Policy Analysis and Management* 1:19-41.

Harrington, W., and A.C. Fisher (1982) Endangered species. Pp. 117-148 in P.R. Portney and R.B. Hass, eds., *Current Issues in Natural Resources Policy*. Washington, D.C.: Resources for the Future.

Harris, R., and R. Sabot (1982) Urban unemployment in LDCs: toward a more general search model. In R. Sabot, ed., *Migration and the Labor Market in Developing Countries*. Boulder, Colo.: Westview Press.

Harris, R., and M. Todaro (1970) Migration, unemployment, and development: a two sector analysis. *American Economic Review* 60:126-142.

Hayami, Y., and V.W. Ruttan (1984) The green revolution: inducement and distribution. *Pakistan Development Review* 23(Spring):38-63.

Hayami, Y., and V.W. Ruttan (1985a) *Agricultural Development: An International Perspective*. Baltimore, Md.: Johns Hopkins University Press.

Hayami, Y., and V.W. Ruttan (1985b) Population Growth and Agricultural Productivity. Background paper prepared for the Working Group on Population Growth and Economic Development, Committee on Population, National Research Council, Washington, D.C.

Henderson, J.V. (1984) General equilibrium modeling of systems of cities. In P. Nijkamp and E. Mills, eds., *Handbooks in Regional and Urban Economics*. New York: North-Holland.

Henderson, J.V. (1985) Industrialization and Urbanization: International Experience. Background paper prepared for the Working Group on Population Growth and Economic Development, Committee on Population, National Research Council, Washington, D.C.

Heyneman, S.P., and W.A. Loxley (1983) The effect of primary-school quality on academic achievement across twenty-nine high- and low-income countries. *American Journal of Sociology* 88(6):1162-1192.

Hinman, C.W. (1984) New crops for arid lands. *Science* 225:1445-1448.

Ingram, G.K. (1980) Land in Perspective: Its Role in the Structure of Cities. Urban and Regional Report 80-9. World Bank, Washington, D.C.

International Labour Organisation (1974) *Sharing in Development*. Geneva: International Labour Organisation.

James, J. (1985) Population and Technical Change in the Manufacturing Sector of Developing Countries. Background paper prepared for the Working Group on Population Growth and Economic Development, Committee on Population, National Research Council, Washington, D.C.

Johnson, D.G. (1974) Population, food, and economic adjustment. *American Statistician* 28(3):89-93.

Johnson, D.G. (1985) *World Commodity Market Situation and Outlook*. Washington, D.C.: American Enterprise Institute.

Jones, G.W. (1971) Effect of population change on the attainment of educational goods in developing countries. Pp. 315-367 in National Academy of Sciences, *Rapid Population Growth: Consequences and Policy Implications*. Baltimore, Md.: Johns Hopkins University Press.

Jones, G.W. (1975) *Population Growth and Education Planning in Developing Nations*. New York: John Wiley and Sons.

Keeley, M.C. (1976) A neoclassical analysis of economic-demographic simulation models. Pp. 25-46 in M.C. Keeley, ed., *Population, Public Policy, and Economic Development*. New York: Praeger.

Kelley, A.C. (1973) Population growth, the dependency rate, and the pace of economic development. *Population Studies* 27:405-414.

Kelley, A.C. (1976) Demographic change and the size of the government sector. *Southern Economic Journal* 43(2):1056-1066.

Kelley, A., and J. Williamson (1984) *What Drives Third World City Growth?* Princeton, N.J.: Princeton University Press.

Khan, A.R. (1984) Population Growth and Access to Land: An Asian Perspective. Paper prepared for the IUSSP Seminar on Population, Food, and Rural Development. New Delhi, India.

King, E.M. (1985) Consequences of Population Pressure in the Family's Welfare. Background paper prepared for the Working Group on Population Growth and Economic Development, Committee on Population, National Research Council, Washington, D.C.

Kirchner, J., J. Drake, G. Ledec, R. Goodland, V. Smil, and H.E. Daly (1984) Carrying Capacity, Population Growth and Sustainable Development. Working Paper No. 690. World Bank, Washington, D.C.

Knight, J.B., and R. Sabot (1982) Land market discrimination in a poor urban economy. *Journal of Development Studies* 19(1):67-87.

Koopmans, T.C. (1974) Proof for a case where discounting advances the doomsday. Pp. 117-120 in *Symposium on the Economics of Exhaustible Resources*.

Krueger, A. (1978) Alternative trade strategies and employment in LDCs. *American Economic Review* 68:270-274.

Kuznets, S. (1967) Population and economic growth. *Proceedings of the American Philosophical Society* 3(3):170-193.

Kuznets, S. (1976) Demographic aspects of the size distribution of income. *Economic Development and Cultural Change* 25(1):1-94.

Lam, D. (1985) Distribution Issues in the Relationship Between Population Growth and Economic Development. Background paper prepared for the Working Group on Population Growth and Economic Development, Committee on Population, National Research Council, Washington, D.C.

Lee, R. (1980) An historical perspective on economic aspects of the population explosion: the case of pre-industrial England. Pp. 517-556 in R.E. Easterlin, ed., *Population and Economic Change in Developing Countries*. Chicago: University of Chicago Press.

Lefebvre, A. (1977) Croissance demographique et progres economique dans les pays en developpment de 1960 a 1974 [Demographic growth and economic progress in developing countries from 1960 to 1974]. *Population* (Paris) 32(6):1287-1293.

Leff, N. (1968) Dependency rates and savings rates. *American Economic Review* 59:886-895.

Leibenstein, H. (1971) The impact of population growth on economic welfare—nontraditional elements. Pp. 175-198 in National Academy of Sciences, *Rapid Population Growth: Consequences and Policy Implications*. Baltimore, Md.: Johns Hopkins University Press.

Leontief, W., J. Koo, S. Nasar, and I. Sohn (1983) *The Future of Nonfuel Minerals in the U.S. and World Economy*. Lexington, Mass.: D.C. Heath.

Lewis, A. (1954) Development with unlimited supplies of labor. *Manchester School of Economics and Social Studies* 20:139-192.

Li, C. (1985) Economic reform brings better life. *Beijing Review* 28(29):15-22.

Linn, J. (1983) *Cities in the Developing World*. New York: Oxford University Press.

MacKellar, F.L., and D.R. Vining, Jr. (1985) Natural Resource Scarcity: A Global Summary. Background paper prepared for the Working Group on Population Growth and Economic Development, Committee on Population, National Research Council, Washington, D.C.

Mason, A. (1985) National Saving Rates and Population Growth: A New Model and New Evidence. Background paper prepared for the Working Group on Population Growth and

Economic Development, Committee on Population, National Research Council, Washington, D.C.

Mazumdar, D. (1984) The rural-urban wage gap migration and the working of urban labor markets. *Indian Economic Review* 18(2):169-198.

Mazumdar, D. (1985) Rural-Urban Migration in Developing Countries. Paper prepared for the Conference on Population Growth, Urbanization, and Urban Policies in the Asia-Pacific Region. East-West Center, Honolulu, Hawaii.

McNicoll, G. (1984) Consequences of rapid population growth: overview and assessment. *Population and Development Review* 10(2):177-240.

Meadows, D.H., D.L. Meadows, J. Randers, and W.W. Behrens III (1972) *The Limits to Growth*. New York: Universe Books.

Mellor, J., and B.F. Johnston (1984) The world food equation: interrelations among development, employment, and food consumption. *Journal of Economic Literature* 12:531-574.

Mensch, B., H. Lentzner, and S. Preston (1985) *Child Mortality Differentials in Developing Countries*. New York: United Nations.

Miller, K.R., J. Furtado, C. de Klemm, J.A. McNeely, N. Muyers, M.E. Soule, and M.C. Trexler (1986) Issues on the preservation of biological diversity. In R. Repetto, ed., *The Global Possible*. World Resources Institute. New Haven, Conn.: Yale University Press.

Mohan, R. (1984) The effect of population growth, the pattern of demand and of technology on the process of urbanization. *Journal of Urban Economics* 15:125-156.

Montgomery, M.A. (1985) The Impacts of Urban Population Growth on Urban Labor Markets and the Costs of Urban Service Delivery: A Review. Background paper prepared for the Working Group on Population Growth and Economic Development, Committee on Population, National Research Council, Washington, D.C.

Mosley, H. (1983) Will Primary Health Care Reduce Infant and Child Mortality? A Critique of Some Current Strategies, with Special Reference to Africa and Asia. Paper prepared for the IUSSP Seminar on Social Policy, Health Policy, and Mortality Prospects. Paris, France.

Mueller, E. (1984) Income, aspirations, and fertility in rural areas of less developed countries. Pp. 121-150 in W.A. Schutjer and C.S. Stokes, eds., *Rural Development and Fertility*. London: Macmillan.

Murnane, R.J. (1981) Interpreting the evidence on school effectiveness. *Teachers College Record* 83:19-35.

Muscat, R. (1984) Carrying Capacity and Rapid Population Growth: Definition, Cases, and Consequences. Working Paper No. 690. World Bank, Washington, D.C.

Myers, N. (1980) *Conversion of Tropical Moist Forests*. Board on Science and Technology for International Development. Washington, D.C.: National Academy Press.

National Academy of Sciences (1971) *Rapid Population Growth: Consequences and Policy Implications*. 2 vols. Baltimore, Md.: Johns Hopkins University Press.

National Research Council (1984) *Changing Climate: Report of the Carbon Dioxide Assessment Committee*. Board on Atmospheric Sciences and Climates. Washington, D.C.: National Academy Press.

Nerlove, M., A. Razin, and E. Sadka (1984) Some Welfare Theoretic Implications of Endogenous Fertility. Paper prepared for the Conference on the Economics of the Family. University of Pennsylvania.

North, D.D., and R.P. Thomas (1973) *The Rise of the Western World: A New Economic History*. Cambridge, England: Cambridge University Press.

Oberai, A. (1978) *Changes in the Structure of Employment with Economic Development*. Geneva: International Labour Organisation.

Phelps, E.S. (1962) The view of investment. *Quarterly Journal of Economics* 76:548-567.

Phelps, E.S. (1968) Population increase. *Canadian Journal of Economics* 1(3):497-518.

Phelps, E.S. (1980) On the increase of technology. Pp. 129-132 in E.S. Phelps, ed., *Studies in Macroeconomic Theory. Vol. 2: Redistribution and Growth.* New York: Academic Press.

Pingali, P.L., and H.P. Binswanger (1984) Population Density and Farming Systems: The Changing Focus of Innovations and Technical Change. Paper prepared for the IUSSP Seminar on Population and Rural Development. New Delhi, India.

Pingali, P.L., and H.P. Binswanger (1985) Population Density and Agricultural Intensification: A Study of the Evolution of Technologies in Tropical Agriculture. Background paper prepared for the Working Group on Population Growth and Economic Development, Committee on Population, National Research Council, Washington, D.C.

Portes, A., and L. Benton (1984) Industrial development and labor force absorption. *Population and Development Review* 10(4):589-612.

Portney, P.R. (1982) Introduction. Pp. 1-13 in P.R. Portney and R.B. Haas, eds., *Current Issues in Natural Resource Policy.* Baltimore, Md.: Johns Hopkins University Press.

Postel, S. (1984) Protecting forests. Pp. 74-94 in L.R. Brown et al., eds., *State of the World.* New York: W.W. Norton & Co.

Potter, J. (1978) Demographic factors and income distribution in Latin America. Pp. 321-337 in *Proceedings, Economic and Demographic Change: Issues for the 1980s.* Helsinki: International Union for the Scientific Study of Population.

Preston, S. (1979) Urban growth in developing countries: a demographic reappraisal. *Population and Development Review* 5(2):195-215.

Psacharopoulos, G. (1981) Returns to education: an updated international comparison. *Comparative Education* 17(3):321-347.

Ram, R., and T.W. Schultz (1979) Life span, health, savings, and productivity. *Economic Development and Cultural Change* 27(3):399-421.

Rempel, H. (1981) *Rural-Urban Labor Migration and Urban Unemployment in Kenya.* Laxenburg, Austria: International Institute for Applied Systems Analysis.

Renaud, B. (1982) *National Urbanization Policy in Developing Countries.* New York: Oxford University Press.

Revelle, R. (1976) The resources available for agriculture. *Scientific American* 235(3):164-179.

Ridker, R.G. (1976) *Population and Development: The Search for Selective Interventions.* Baltimore, Md.: Johns Hopkins University Press.

Rodgers, G. (1984) *Poverty and Population: Approaches and Evidence.* Geneva: International Labour Organisation.

Rosenzweig, M., and K.I. Wolpin (1980) Testing the quantity-quality fertility model: the use of twins as a natural experiment. *Econometrica* 48(1):227-240.

Rosenzweig, M., H.P. Binswanger, and J. McIntyre (1984) From Land-Abundance to Land-Scarcity: The Effects of Population Growth on Production Relations in Agrarian Economies. Paper prepared for the IUSSP Conference on Population, Food, and Rural Development. New Delhi, India.

Ruttan, V.W., and Hayami, Y. (1984) Induced innovation model of agricultural development. Pp. 59-74 in C.K. Eicher and J. Staatz, eds., *Agricultural Development in the Third World.* Baltimore, Md.: Johns Hopkins University Press.

Sabolo, Y. (1975) Employment and unemployment, 1960-1990. *International Labour Review* 112(6):401-417.

Schultz, T.P. (1971) Rural-urban migration in Colombia. *Review of Economics and Statistics* 53:157-163.

Schultz, T.P. (1985) School Expenditures and Enrollment, 1960-1980: The Effects of Income Prices and Population Growth. Background paper prepared for the Working Group on Population Growth and Economic Development, Committee on Population, National Research Council, Washington, D.C.

Schultz, T.W. (1979) Investment in population quality in low income countries. Pp. 339-360 in P.M. Haieser, ed., *World Population and Development: Challenges and Prospects.* Syracuse, N.Y.: Syracuse University Press.

Schutjer, W.A., and C.S. Stokes, eds. (1984) *Rural Development and Fertility.* London: Macmillan.

Sedjo, R.A., and M.C. Clawson (1984) Global forests. Pp. 128-170 in J.L. Simon and H. Kahn, eds., *The Resourceful Earth: A Response to Global 2000.* New York: Basil Blackwell.

Sen, A. (1981) *Poverty and Famines: An Essay on Entitlement and Deprivation.* Oxford, England: Clarendon Press.

Simmons, J., and L. Alexander (1978) The determinants of school achievement in developing countries: a review of the research. *Economic Development and Cultural Change* 26(2):341-357.

Simon, J.L. (1975) The positive effect of population growth on agricultural saving in irrigation systems. *Review of Economics and Statistics* 57:71-79.

Simon, J.L. (1977) *The Economics of Population Growth.* Princeton, N.J.: Princeton University Press.

Simon, J.L. (1981) *The Ultimate Resource.* Princeton, N.J.: Princeton University Press.

Simon, J.L., and R. Gobin (1980) The relationship between population and economic growth in LDCs. *Research in Population Economics* 2:215-234.

Simon, J.L., and H. Kahn, eds. (1984) *The Resourceful Earth: A Response to Global 2000.* New York: Basil Blackwell.

Simon, J.L., and A.M. Pilarski (1979) The effect of population growth upon the quantity of education children receive. *Review of Economics and Statistics* 61(4):572-584.

Simon, J.L., and G. Steinman (1981) Population growth and Phelps' technical progress model: interpretation and generalization. Pp. 239-254 in J.L. Simon and P. Lindert, eds., *Research in Population Economics,* Vol. 3. Greenwich, Conn.: JAI Press.

Simon, J.L., and A. Wildavsky (1984) On species loss, the absence of data, and risks to humanity. Pp. 171-183 in J.L. Simon and H. Kahn, eds., *The Resourceful Earth: A Response to Global 2000.* New York: Basil Blackwell.

Slade, M.E. (1982) Trends in natural resource commodity prices: an analysis of the time domain. *Journal of Environmental Economics and Management* 9:122-137.

Slade, M.E. (1985) Natural Resources, Population Growth, and Economic Well-Being. Background paper prepared for the Working Group on Population Growth and Economic Development, Committee on Population, National Research Council, Washington, D.C.

Slicher van Bath, B.H. (1963) *The Agrarian History of Western Europe, A.D. 500-1850.* London: Edward Arnold.

Smil, V. (1984) *The Bad Earth: Environmental Degradation in China.* Armonk, N.Y.: Sharpe.

Smith, V.K., and J.V. Krutilla (1979) Resource and environmental constraints to growth. *American Journal of Agricultural Economics* 61(3):395-408.

Solow, R. (1956) A contribution to the theory of economic growth. *Quarterly Journal of Economics* 70:65-90.

Squire, L. (1981) *Employment Policy in Developing Countries.* New York: Oxford University Press.

Srinivasan, T.N. (1985) Population, Food, and Rural Development. Background paper prepared for the Working Group on Population Growth and Economic Development,

Committee on Population, National Research Council, Washington, D.C.

Srinivasan, T.N., and P.K. Bardhan (1974) *Poverty and Income Distribution in India.* Calcutta: Statistical Publishing Society.

Standing, G. (1984) Labour Supply and Development Policies: A Perspective. Paper prepared for the Conference on Population Growth and Labor Absorption in the Developing World (Rockefeller Foundation). Bellagio, Italy.

Starrett, D. (1972) On golden rules, the "biological rate of interest" and competitive inefficiency. *Journal of Political Economy* 80:276-291.

Stern, J., and J. Lewis (1980) Employment Patterns and Income Growth. Working Paper No. 419. World Bank, Washington, D.C.

Stiglitz, J.E. (1979) A neoclassical analysis of the economics of natural resources. In V.K. Smith, ed., *Scarcity and Growth Reconsidered.* Baltimore, Md.: Johns Hopkins University Press.

Stolnitz, G.J. (1984) Urbanization and Rural-to-Urban Migration in Relation to LDC Fertility. Fertility Determinants Group/Futures Group Study for the Agency for International Development. Indiana University, Bloomington.

Strauss, J. (1985) Does Better Nutrition Raise Farm Productivity? Unpublished manuscript. Yale University.

Tan, J.P., and M. Haines (1983) Schooling and the Demand for Children: Historical Perspectives. Background paper prepared for the *1984 World Development Report.* World Bank, Washington, D.C.

Terhune, K.W. (1974) *A Review of the Actual and Expected Consequences of Family Size.* Buffalo, N.Y.: Calspan Corp.

Tobin, J. (1967) Life cycle saving and balanced economic growth. Pp. 231-256 in W. Fellner, ed., *Ten Economic Studies in the Tradition of Irving Fisher.* New York: Wiley Press.

Todaro, M. (1969) A model of labor migration and urban unemployment in less developed countries. *American Economic Review* 59:393-423.

Todaro, M. (1980) Internal migration in developing countries: a survey. In R. Easterlin, ed., *Population and Economic Change in Developing Countries.* Chicago: University of Chicago Press.

Todaro, M., and J. Stilkind (1981) *City Bias and Rural Neglect: The Dilemma of Urban Development.* New York: The Population Council.

Trussell, J., and A.R. Pebley (1984) The Potential Impact of Changes in Fertility on Infant, Child, and Maternal Mortality. Unpublished manuscript. Princeton University.

United Nations, Population Division (1980) *Patterns of Urban and Rural Population Growth.* New York: United Nations.

United Nations, Department of Technical Cooperation for Development (1984) *Report of the International Conference on Population 1984.* New York: United Nations.

United Nations (1985) *Migration, Population Growth and Employment in Metropolitan Areas of Selected Developing Countries.* New York: United Nations.

U.S. Department of Agriculture, Economic Research Service (1985) *China: Outlook and Situation.* Report RS 85-5. Washington, D.C.: U.S. Department of Agriculture.

Usher, D. (1973) An imputation to the measure of economic growth for changes in life expectancy. In M. Moss, ed., *The Measurement of Economic and Social Performance.* New York: National Bureau of Economic Research.

Wattenberg, B., and K. Zinsmeister (1985) *Are World Population Trends a Problem?* Washington, D.C.: American Enterprise Institute.

Westoff, C.F. (1978) The unmet need for birth control in five Asian countries. *International Family Planning Perspectives* 4(1):9-17.

Williamson, J.G., and P.H. Lindert (1980) *American Inequality: A Macroeconomic History.* New York: Academic Press.

Willis, R.J. (1985) Externalities and Population. Background paper prepared for the Working Group on Population Growth and Economic Development, Committee on Population, National Research Council, Washington, D.C.

Woodwell, G.M., J.E. Hobbie, R.A. Houghton, J.M. Melillo, B. Moore, B.J. Peterson, and G.R. Shaver (1983) Global deforestation: contribution to atmospheric carbon dioxide. *Science* 222:1081-1088.

World Bank (1974) *Population Policies and Economic Development.* Baltimore, Md.: Johns Hopkins University Press.

World Bank (1983a) *World Tables. Economic Data*, Vol. I. Baltimore, Md.: Johns Hopkins University Press.

World Bank (1983b) *World Tables. Social Data*, Vol. II. Baltimore, Md.: Johns Hopkins University Press.

World Bank (1984) *World Development Report.* Washington, D.C.: World Bank.

World Health Organization (1975) *Fifth Report on the World Health Situation.* Official Records of the World Health Organization, N. 225. Geneva: World Health Organization.

World Meteorological Organization (1983) Population and Climate. Paper presented at the International Conference on Population. Geneva.

Wray, J.D. (1971) Population pressure on families: family size and child spacing. Pp. 403-461 in National Academy of Sciences, *Rapid Population Growth: Consequences and Policy Implications.* Baltimore, Md.: Johns Hopkins University Press.

Yap, L. (1977) The attraction of cities: a review of the migration literature. *Journal of Development Economics* 4(3):239-264.

Index